Using Action Research to Foster Positive Social Values

Jean Benton

ScarecrowEducation
Lanham, Maryland • Toronto • Oxford
2005

Published in the United States of America
by ScarecrowEducation
An imprint of The Rowman & Littlefield Publishing Group, Inc.
4501 Forbes Boulevard, Suite 200, Lanham, Maryland 20706
www.scarecroweducation.com

PO Box 317
Oxford
OX2 9RU, UK

Copyright © 2005 by Jean Benton

All rights reserved. No part of this publication may be reproduced, stored in a retrieval system, or transmitted in any form or by any means, electronic, mechanical, photocopying, recording, or otherwise, without the prior permission of the publisher.

British Library Cataloguing in Publication Information Available

Library of Congress Cataloging-in-Publication Data

Benton, Jean, 1943–
  Using action research to foster positive social values / Jean Benton.
    p. cm.
  Includes bibliographical references and index.
  ISBN 1-57886-210-8 (pbk. : alk. paper)
  1. Moral education—United States. 2. Social values—Study and teaching—United States. 3. School violence—United States—Prevention. 4. Action research in education—United States. I. Title.

LC311.B46 2005
370.11'4—dc22
                                                            2004022656

∞^{TM} The paper used in this publication meets the minimum requirements of American National Standard for Information Sciences—Permanence of Paper for Printed Library Materials, ANSI/NISO Z39.48-1992.
Manufactured in the United States of America.

Contents

Introduction		v
Part I	**Basis for Disruptive Behavior**	
1	Formation of American Values and the Search for Identity	3
2	Families	11
3	Religion and Spirituality	27
4	Community	39
Part II	**Using Classroom Research to Foster Positive Values**	
5	What Is Action Research?	51
6	Formulating Plans to Develop Peaceful Classrooms	61
Part III	**Case Studies in Best Practices**	
7	Conflict Resolution and Peer Mediation	73
8	Peer Learning, Paired Learning, and Positive Interdependence	85
9	Cooperative Groups	99
10	Parent–Child–Community Collaboration	115

Conclusion 123

Index 125

About the Author 127

Introduction

In light of the recent escalation of school violence, teachers have been increasingly concerned with how to handle pupils who are disruptive, disrespectful, and unable to interact with their classmates in a positive social manner. It has become a challenge for teachers to foster positive social values in their classrooms and find a way to internalize these processes in their teaching practice. This book helps teachers reduce disruptive and violent behavior in the classroom. When such behavior occurs, it deprives all children of a quality education and blocks teachers from being able to deliver programs that provide academic success.

The text presents teachers with tools to develop positive social skills in school-aged children, including case studies that assist teachers in identifying best practices in promoting positive social interaction. Another tool is action research, that is, classroom inquiry, which provides teachers with a process to solve these social problems, and where teachers can design and carry out interventions specific to their needs. Therefore, the combination of acquiring a knowledge base of best practices and the use and application of the action research process offers the potential of transforming the disruptive behaviors of students into caring, cooperative environments in schools.

The first chapter traces the formation of American values and how these values have shifted from a society where traditional patterns of life were passed down from generation to generation to a transmission of cultural values that nurtures competitiveness, individualism, and materialism, as well as a mass media youth culture. The topics that this chapter grapple with are how the growth in nonmainstream cultures will continue to further influence cultural values and behaviors, what new paradigms for cultural transmission will take hold in an era of globalization and diversification of society, and how these will influence school culture and teachers' abilities to produce effective classroom climates.

Chapter 2 examines the sources of behavior from the perspective of parents and parenting styles, both in mainstream families and families of color. Within mainstream society, there are several different parenting styles, some of which are more successful than others. But complicating this is the parenting styles of minority parents, who raise successful children through a variety of parenting patterns. It is therefore necessary that the classroom teacher know and understand the parenting-style differences among various ethnic groups and how to effectively discipline children from a range of cultural backgrounds.

Sources of behavior from the perspective of religion and spirituality and how religions promote certain types of parenting styles are investigated in chapter 3. The religious or spiritual disposition of parents has been found to be importantly related to self-reported parenting styles. Based on what parenting styles are most successful for a specific ethnic group, the resulting behavior in children could be beneficial or detrimental. Again, teachers, as well as parents, need to know how religious orientation can affect children's outcomes in school and society.

The importance of community is examined in chapter 4 to help teachers find ways to build community among their students' families so peaceful communities can emerge where violence previously reigned. Key to building these communities is the development and use of social capital. A case study in school–parent–community collaboration in part III shows just how powerful this concept is in creating children who can develop positive social and interpersonal skills for success in school.

Part II provides teachers with the processes and tools to develop successful classrooms and practice when children practice peaceful interactions. Chapter 5 lays out the process of action research through an easy and discernible method of examining and reflecting on classroom practices. The chapter provides an explanation at each stage of the process, identifying the concern, collecting information, designing and implementing an intervention, collecting and analyzing results, evaluating and assessing the effectiveness of the intervention, reflecting on the process, and identifying a new or continuing concern. Reflective questions are also included at each stage to help teachers focus on the issue that they want to resolve. The delineation of the process helps teachers get started on this important pedagogy for their classrooms, but it is part III that shows the process at work in real classroom settings.

Chapter 6 examines various approaches to reducing violence, including peace-keeping, peace-making, and peace-building methods. Peace-making activities—conflict resolution and peer mediation—have been proven to be the most successful in reducing violence in a variety of contexts. These activities are also the kinds of classroom pedagogy that foster democratic classrooms, for example, cooperative groups, peer and paired interdependence, and class meetings. The administration must commit to a vision of peaceful schools and provide for democratic, site-based management, where all staff have a say in how the school is to be administered and parents and the community are part of the process.

Part III presents four case studies of teachers using action research to solve issues of disruptive and violent behavior. The case study in chapter 7 focuses on conflict resolution and peer mediation pedagogies. The teacher in this classroom found that she was spending more time dealing with conflicts than teaching. Through her action research project, she instituted daily lessons that taught children to deal with conflict through a variety of teaching approaches, techniques, and media. She found that over the course of the project students had learned how to deal with conflict through reflective thought and had gained greater identity of themselves and how others viewed their behavior.

Chapter 8 provides teachers with insight into how another teacher helped children learn how to support one another through an array of activities focused on developing peer and paired interdependence. She found that the children became much more aware of the need to provide assistance, and they internalized the strategies and transferred them to other activities in the classroom by helping friends perform various tasks, improving the total social climate of the classroom.

Chapter 9 details one teacher's attempt to develop groups to increase cooperation, respect, and tolerance among her students. This teacher instituted a parallel process of having students learn social skills through role-play and modeling by the teacher, and then applying these new skills in cooperative group settings. However, the findings showed an increase in both tolerant and intolerant behavior, which indicated that the intervention was not totally successful. The data also provided the teacher with further direction for the next cycle of research.

Chapter 10 moves the framework for action research outside the school and into the community. The teacher in this case study went to a family resource center to assist her students in developing more effective social, life, and academic skills through the implementation of a mentoring program that utilized seniors from the community. Post-intervention data found that there were significant gains in all three areas, but the most significant were made in life and social skills.

I hope this book will encourage teachers to probe into areas of their pedagogy that they want to refine and make more effective through action research. As can be seen through the cases in this book, ordinary teachers were able to accomplish extraordinary things with their students and teaching practice. As more and more teachers develop their teaching practice in this way, it is also hoped that teachers will take the lead in defining effective classroom practice.

Part I

BASIS FOR DISRUPTIVE BEHAVIOR

CHAPTER 1

Formation of American Values and the Search for Identity

One aspect of disruptive behavior has its roots in the family–church–community paradigm that first-generation European immigrants brought to America. This model of cultural transmission held a tight rein on the moral, ethical, and educational training of children. Its basis was the extended family, which included a wide range of dependents: children well beyond the age of maturity, as well as nephews, nieces, cousins, and servants, in some cases. Families, therefore, were the primary agencies of socialization of the child. "Not only did the family introduce [the child] to the basic forms of civilized living, but it shaped his attitudes, formed his patterns of behavior, endowed him with manners and morals" (Bailyn, 1972). The family also served as the first educator, providing the initial steps of apprenticeship into the family trade. "Like other forms of bonded servitude, it was a condition of dependency, a childlike state of legal incompetence, in which the master's role, and responsibilities, was indistinguishable from the father's" (Bailyn, 1972). Thus, the family and the apprenticeship model created a formula of delayed responsibility for young people.

While the family was the basis for the child's moral beginnings, it was the church and the community that built on these basic family values. In early America, communities were small and slow to change. Most everyone in these small towns was related to someone in one way or another, thus extending the family into the community as well. "It was at times difficult for the child to know where the family left off and the greater society began" (Bailyn, 1972). It was the church, though, that was more explicit in its educative function.

> It furthered the introduction of the child to society by instructing him in the system of thought and imagery, which underlay the culture's values and aims. It provided the highest sanctions for the accepted forms of behavior, and brought the child into close relationship with the intangible loyalties, the ethos and highest principles of the society in which he lived. (Bailyn, 1972)

So it was, then, that the family, the community, and the church transmitted the culture from generation to generation, or at least until these European settlers came to America.

This cultural transmission pattern quickly unraveled once the settlers arrived. As community elders were faced with new and daunting problems in a frontier wilderness that did not fit the patterns of their cultural upbringing, they had to change their way of life and the underlying value system that provided their security in a once-stable world. Roles of adults changed. Once able to pass on skills and knowledge and rely on prescriptive solutions, they were now working as menial laborers to harvest crops, construct new buildings, and defend the community against incursions in order to survive in this new land. It took only a single generation for the once-familiar patterns of family and community life to change altogether. Young people, now laboring alongside their parents, were much more flexible to adapt to their new environments.

> The young—less bound by prescriptive memories, more adaptable, more vigorous—stood at advantage. Learning faster, they came to see the world more familiarly, to concede more readily to unexpected necessities, to sense more accurately the phasing of a new life. They, not their parents, became the effective guides to a new world, and they thereby gained a strange, anomalous authority difficult to accommodate within the ancient structure of family life. (Bailyn, 1972)

Thus, the traditional patterns of passing down wisdom from generation to generation and providing the moral and ethical supports for young people became eroded, as did the influence of the elders in the community, which further led to an increasingly horizontal flow of cultural transmission, from one youth to another.

This, then, was the beginning of the shift from a society where traditional patterns of life were passed down from generation to generation from within the family and from community elders. As the country continued to be settled, more family upheaval occurred. The push to tame the boundless wilderness that stretched for three thousand miles westward was irresistible, and it was the young people who were forging the way. As they arrived in new territories and settled towns, there were no community elders to set the moral and ethical standards. These young people invented life and its rules as they went along. The constant uprooting of families to move again and again also continued to erode the once-stable lifestyles known to the early European settlers. Thus, the flow of cultural values was once and forever changed.

These American assumptions and values about how one is to live life were set early in our history. It is seen not only in the way Americans approach work, play, and achievement but also in the way we relate to others, the way we view the world, and the way we view ourselves. If there had not been a wilderness to tame, Americans would not be defining ourselves as we now do.

Several aspects of each of these valuing orientations are important to further understand how our current value system was formed and why current issues of disruptive behavior manifest themselves the way they do. As a result of our frontier experiences, we approach life from an aspect of "doing," a dominant activity for Americans. We believe that being incessantly busy is worthwhile and that achievement is important, as are visible accomplishments and the external measurement of them. We approach work and play with equal seriousness, and through our efforts, we believe we will succeed in both (Stewart, 1971). Because achievement is so important, we invent ways of becoming more successful, more competitive, and more cutting edge. This is manifested in our current fascination with using technology to buy and sell information. Yet, of all these attributes, the most important is competition. Competition is the primary method among Americans of motivating members of a group and as a culture (Potter, 1954; Hofstede, 1984). Americans, with their individualism and ideas on achieving, respond well to this technique.

> During their history, Americans have exploited their physical environment as if it were unlimited. The vastness of the land and the opulence of its resources no doubt strengthened the pre-existing belief that the

limits to achievement are measured within the individual. (Stewart, 1971)

Another aspect of American culture that can be attributed to the changing circumstances of a frontier society is the way we relate to others. We have numerous personal relationships, marked by friendliness and informality, yet rarely deep or lasting. Friends and membership groups change easily as an American shifts status or locale; consequently, social life lacks both permanence and depth (Kluckhohn, 1958). Still further is the notion of equality, another frontier equalizer, to which Americans ascribe, especially with regard to social class, although its application is somewhat uneven given our past history of racial issues in this country. Because of this notion of equality, we also feel comfortable being direct with people and confronting issues head-on. Stewart (1971) found that in combining our love of competition with our friendliness and informality, we tend to cooperate among individuals and groups to get things done. But this cooperation is not group oriented. While Americans would accept the goals of the group, they would also expect to pursue their own personal goals within the context of the group.

Thus, individualism and individuality constitute another value important to understanding the issues of social behavior. Hofstede (1984) found Americans to be the most individualistic of all cultures; personal time, freedom, and challenge were work goals most positively correlated to this individualism.

Individualism, materialism, and competitiveness are nurtured in us (Clark, 1989). American children are encouraged to be autonomous at an early age. In schools, we expect them to "do their own work."

> It is implicitly accepted that each child or person should be encouraged to decide for himself, develop his own opinions, solve his own problems, have his own things, and, in general, learn to view the world from the point of view of the self. The American is not expected to bow to the wishes of authority, be it vested in family, traditions, or some organization. (Stewart, 1971)

This individuality, though, was never unfettered. There has always been pressure to conform to social norms, but these acceptable standards of behavior have been defined more and more by the horizontal transmission of cultural values. This flow, which began its shift in early American history, has continued to gain strength as Americans continue to define themselves through a youth-culture framework. Looking young and youthfully vibrant is important. The materialistic consumption of clothes, cars, and every aspect of the culture panders to this value. Each generation of Americans is committed to the rediscovery of self and the claiming of it as its own invention (e.g., Generation X). To reinforce their uniqueness, it becomes necessary to create social identities different from the previous generation. Thus, "the development and exploration of the self takes place in the cultural islands" (Stewart, 1971).

One other aspect of the way we view ourselves is relevant to this discussion of social values. There has been a shift in the importance of personal values at the expense of more publicly standardized group values, whether from an organization, community, social class, profession, minority, or interest group (Kluckhohn, 1958). This shifting value can be found in the numerous group activities available to young people that, in many cases, fill their entire daily calendars. Little league, youth football, soccer and cheerleading camps, ballet, church groups, computer classes, and endless other variations of these groups subsume the daily lives of young people. There seems to be little time to explore one's own identity, or even the desire to do so. This has created the breakdown of barriers to one's own uniqueness. Examples include the blurring of lines of body image, dress, appearance, and behavior between sexes or the blurring of what is acceptable moral and ethical behavior as seen in shows such as *Beavis and Butthead*, *The Simpsons*, and *South Park*. Once-clear notions of social boundaries of respect and positive interactions with others have continued to erode.

According to Cavalli-Sforza, Feldman, Chen, and Dornbusch (1982), the rate of cultural transmission fluctuates most rapidly when cultural transmitters are teachers, other youths, social leaders, and mass media. In the American cultural context, this means that the parent-to-child (vertical) transmission is less influential than that of child to child (horizontal) and nonrelated adults and mass media to child, since a one-to-many transmission takes longer to occur. As each generation attempts to define itself, the rate of cultural transmission takes on increasing importance.

Values transmitted from many to one, such as social class influences, have the lowest rate of cultural change and therefore would not help a generation reinvent itself. On the other hand, values transmitted from one to many would much more conveniently adapt to the creation of a new set of valuing/social norms by a new generation. Thus, parents' ability to control their children will continue to erode, while the mass media, other youths, and community leaders will build momentum with their messages.

While these perspectives generally describe mainstream culture, it is also necessary to add to this mix the influences of other groups and their belief systems. As the nonmainstream culture grows in population, the cultural patterns of other groups—Hispanic, Native American, African American, Asian, Middle Eastern—are now being integrated into mainstream culture. These groups, generally, have cultural patterns much different from mainstream America. Significantly different are the issues of family obligation, filial duty, and views of self, the world, and others that could signal a shift in how current values are transmitted and developed. It is also possible that the family–community–church pattern in which nonmainstream groups are highly grounded could return, but in another configuration, one of non-Western thinking and action. This could possibly be a new paradigm to consider in the debate about how to instill positive social values in our young people.

Further still, we need to consider the current movement toward globalization in all areas of the economy, politics, and social life. Several issues of importance to our topic emerge here. While the United States exerts its influence internationally, the country's search for identity continues to turn inward. For generations our conquering of new frontiers propelled us to develop an "us and them" mentality, one that pitted man against nature. With the Cold War over and space—the last frontier—already being conquered, the "us and them" is now society and ourselves. Also, if corporations continue to move families around not only the country but also the world, it could impede any sense of stability that the mainstream culture originally had or that the immigrant groups bring to American culture. Finally, we need to take seriously the issue of globalization and, therefore, homogenization of cultures in the world. Of course, those cultures buying and selling information (e.g., Americans) will hold an advantage in spreading their cultural values, but nevertheless, many other cultures are strong economically (e.g., Japan), which has already had an impact on American/Western thinking and will most likely continue to do so. It remains to be seen, though, which corporate culture will dominate in the global economy. Will it be a Western model of thinking, doing, and relating, which includes an ever-growing European Union; will it be a non-Western model; or will it be an integration of both valuing systems? Whichever takes hold, the ethos of these cultural values will set the valuing system for the future of the entire world.

REFERENCES

Bailyn, B. (1972). *Education in the forming of American society.* New York: Norton.

Cavalli-Sforza, L. L., Feldman, M. W., Chen, K. H., & Dornbusch, S. M. (1982). Theory and observation in cultural transmission. *Science, 1,* 19–27.

Clark, M. E. (1989). *Ariadne's thread: The search for new modes of thinking.* New York: St. Martin's.

Hofstede, G. (1984). *Culture's consequences: International differences in work-related values.* London: Sage.

Kluckhohn, C. (1958). The evolution of contemporary American values. *Daedalus, 87,* 2.

Potter, D. M. (1954). *People of plenty: Economic abundance and the American character.* Chicago: University of Chicago Press.

Stewart, E. (1971). *American cultural patterns: A cross-cultural perspective.* University of Pittsburgh: Regional Council for International Education.

CHAPTER 2
Families

Disrespectful and disruptive pupils who overstep the social boundaries of constructive interaction are operating on very low levels of moral reasoning, according to Kohlberg and Candee (1984). They found that moral thinking could be advanced educationally if one were to use social interaction, cognitive conflict, a positive moral atmosphere, and democratic participation. Through social experiences that produce cognitive conflict, children are provided opportunities to take the perspectives of others and thus take ownership of the situation, which further assists teachers in establishing democratic classroom processes and pupil empowerment.

As seen in chapter 1, mainstream families were once part of the three-part support system (family, church, and community) that provided opportunities for socially constructive interaction with family and community. It was a time when grandparents, aunts, uncles, and older siblings all shared in the raising of a child. This paradigm has mostly fallen away from mainstream culture but is still widely seen in other cultures. What, then, are these values, practices, and interactions that families of mainstream culture once had and that other cultures, to a large extent, still possess? What current mainstream family practices enhance children's chances for success?

PARENTING STYLES

Baumrind (1966, 1971, 1991) identified three major parenting styles: *authoritarian*, *permissive*, and *authoritative*; Maccoby and Martin (1983) later added a fourth: *uninvolved*. Parents who are *authoritarian* are generally punitive. They focus on gaining a child's obedience to parental demands rather than responding to the demands of the child; they do not encourage verbal interaction. Parents who are *permissive* make few demands on their children, yet these parents are responsive. They do not set appropriate limits on their children's behavior and use little punishment. Parents who are *authoritative* fall between authoritarian and permissive parenting styles. They are flexible and responsive to their children's needs yet still enforce reasonable standards of conduct. Parents who are *uninvolved* do not set limits for their children and are unresponsive to their children's needs. See figure 2.1 for an overview of the four different parenting styles.

Effects of Different Parenting Styles

Studies have shown that the most effective parenting style is authoritative, but in relation to mainstream culture only. Steinberg, Lamborn, Darling, Mounts, and Dronbusch (1994) found the following positive behavior outcomes associated with authoritative parenting: increased competence, autonomy, and self-esteem; better problem-solving skills, academic performance, and peer relations; more self-reliance; and less deviance or aggressive behavior.

Authoritarian-style parenting in mainstream culture leads to negative behavioral outcomes. Hart, Olsen, Robinson, and Mandleco (1997), Rubin, Stewart, and Chen (1994), and Steinberg et al. (1994) found that parents who are authoritarian produce children who are aggressive and

	HIGH CONTROL and DEMANDING		
HIGH WARMTH and RESPONSIVENESS	Authoritative	Authoritarian	LOW WARMTH and RESPONSIVENESS
	Permissive	Uninvolved	
	LOW CONTROL and UNDEMANDING		

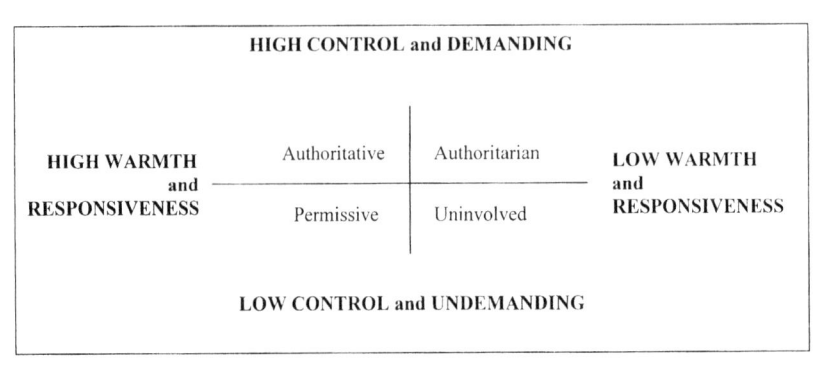

Figure 2.1. Parenting Styles

who lack self-esteem. These children demonstrate decreased emotional functioning and little self-confidence in their academic and social capabilities, as well as later delinquent behavior. Permissive-style parenting is also linked to aggression and delinquent behavior since parents of this type are often lax in supervising their children and in many ways are neglectful and indifferent to their children (Haapasalo & Tremblay, 1994). Hart et al. reported that children from homes with permissive-style parents often display emotional, impulsive, and nonconformist behaviors; school misconduct is common, as well as drug and alcohol use. Wasserman, Miller, Pinner, and Jaramillo (1996) found that when problem behavior is ignored, it worsens or is at least maintained.

Parenting Styles of Minority Parents

Parenting styles that may be considered less than optimal in one culture may be very effective in another. Not as much research exists about the parenting styles from cultural backgrounds other than European American. Therefore, the research reported here provides a direction for understanding the ways in which parents of color produce healthy children. These findings also suggest that in schools where mainstream teachers use their white middle-class parenting styles to teach children of color, a mismatch of parenting styles could exist, which further impacts potential success for children of color.

One study done on a small sample of Hispanic, bi-ethnic, and European American families found some overlap in parenting styles but also some unique features of Hispanic culture that differ from mainstream culture. Boys from European American and bi-ethnic families show clinical levels of behavior problems when they come from hierarchical (authoritarian) and permissive homes, but only lax or inconsistent parenting creates dysfunction in Hispanic families (Lindahl & Malik, 1999). This supports Alvirez and Bean's (1976) findings that underscore the importance and relevance of interdependence in Hispanic families in producing well-adjusted children. Other studies found that Puerto Rican parents display a higher level of nurturance, responsiveness, and consistency with their children than do African American parents (Fagan, 2000). Latino parents often use verbal and physical expressions of parental affection and nurturance (Escovar & Lazarus,

1982), and Latino parents, while structured, frequently use directives, modeling, and visual cues in teaching tasks (Vargas, 1991). These studies indicate that while Latino parents are directive, they do not fit the stereotypical pattern of authoritarian parents since there are also high levels of nurturance and interdependence present.

African American parents show still further variation in parenting behavior. Demo (2000) reports that many African American children's home lives are characterized by substantial diversity and fluidity in family structure, where they are raised by both parents and nonparents and by multiple generations, which leads to close, supportive relationships among the children, their mothers, and grandmothers. African American parents have also been found to use a strict parenting style where a great deal of emphasis is placed on respect for authority, yet they also display high levels of support and expression of emotions (Bartz & Levine, 1978; Rashid, 1985; Taylor, Chatters, Tucker, & Lewis, 1990).

Variations in Mother–Father Parenting Styles among Cultures

Russell et al. (1998) and Smetana (1995) found that white middle-class mothers use more authoritative parenting styles than do fathers, whereas fathers use more authoritarian and permissive styles than do mothers. Studies done with African American and Latino families discovered that successful mother–father parenting styles do not correlate with white parenting styles. McAdoo (1979, 1981) found that African American fathers are nurturing, loving, and sensitive to their children's needs; Bartz and Levine (1978) found that except for one measure—egalitarianism—there are no significant differences in the way Mexican mothers and fathers relate to their children. Asian Indian mothers are the primary caregivers and nurturers, while fathers—perceived as dominant and stern—are to be feared (Kakar, 1978; Ross, 1967).

In Chinese families, adolescent children perceive mothers and fathers as having differing styles of parenting. They perceive fathers to be harsh, less responsive, and less demanding. Mothers are perceived as more concerned and responsive than are fathers. Cultural factors cited as contributing to these findings include emotions, punishment, and role. Chinese men, discouraged from expressing their emotions, are considered the persons who administer corporal punishment as well as take care of things outside the family (Shek, 2000). While changes are taking place in Chinese parenting, firm, coercive discipline is still the dominant norm of parenting (Abbott, Zheng, & Meredith, 1992), and while parents in China believe they are adopting authoritative parenting styles, they are still seen by their children as being authoritarian (Quoss & Wen, 1995). It was also discovered that the more authoritarian the parents, the better the children perceived their overall relationship, yet the children were dissatisfied with the family rules and decision-making processes. The lack of communication between Chinese boys and girls and their fathers also differs from Western culture, where it has been found that adolescent females report having a better relationship with their mothers, and adolescent boys with both parents (Youniss and Smollar, 1985).

Therefore, all parents should definitely be kept aware of the importance of their roles, be encouraged to take on the parenting style that best expresses their cultural values, and continue to develop and maintain this important role in their children's lives. Teachers should allow for these differences in the classroom by understanding and utilizing the discipline style that would most closely match the parenting style. Just as all children in a class will not be reading at the same level, neither should the teacher expect that one discipline style will fit all students. Teachers need to work closely with parents to support and maintain the preferred parenting style of the parents.

Parenting Styles and the Extended Family

Many traditional patterns of life have fallen away to modernization, urbanization, and globalization. The continual upheaval of families either moving or being moved by their employers to new locations, especially to urban areas; the push toward higher levels of education as a necessity for economic well-being; and the increase in life expectancy have created stresses on families that, in the past, were unknown. With the increased movement of people, the once-familiar pattern of extended family support has eroded, especially in mainstream families. However, intergenerational relationships and interactions are still apparent in all types of families, although they are manifested differently depending on race, ethnicity, and social class.

Hispanics have generally originated from cultures with strong patriarchal and European aspects of family life (Billingsley, 1968). Characteristics of Hispanics present the image of strong commitment to family, male responsibility for the family, and authoritarian parenting (Alvirez & Bean, 1976; Baca Zinn, 1982, 1994; Carrasquillo, 1994; Mirande, 1979, 1985). Despite the authoritarian role of the male head of the household, Hispanic families are also characterized as self-reliant and interdependent. Thus, this authoritarian parenting style is modified through strong family interdependence, which provides the same sort of support structures as seen in authoritative parenting.

In Native American culture, extended family is manifested in the concept of community. American Indian families differ from other extended family units in the Western world through the structural openness and village-type characteristic of tribes and clans (Woods, 1996). Living in a tribal community is much like living in a small town where everyone knows and watches out for everyone else. This is especially true of Native Americans who are closely interwoven through blood, marriage, and longtime associations (Horejsi, Craig, & Pablo, 1992). Personal relationships are strengths of the American Indian family. At the center are their relationships with and respect for nature and a creator, as well as respect for elders and children, which forms the foundation of discipline and authority (Woods, 1996).

> Native Americans are typically part of an extended family structure. Aunts may be called "mother," uncles may be called "father." An individual's cousins may be treated as brothers and sisters. Grandparents are often key decision-makers and frequently play a central role in the parenting of young children. Other members of the extended family usually assume child care responsibilities and may discipline children. (Horejsi, Craig, & Pablo, 1992)

While this is the traditional structure of Native American families, many intergenerational family structures were torn apart by the legacy of boarding schools.

> The boarding schools not only destroyed or distorted the intergenerational [cultural] transmission of family and parenting knowledge and be-

havior, but they also introduced new and dysfunctional behaviors, such as the use of severe punishment in child-rearing. Parents who had as children been spanked and hit while attending boarding school responded similarly to their own children. Before the boarding school era, the use of physical discipline was uncommon in most tribes. (Horejsi, Craig, & Pablo, 1992)

Japanese families display an interdependent kinship network of solidarity and sociability, which encourages indebtedness and obligatory patterns of interaction (Hutter, 1988). Grandparents usually live with their adult children and grandchildren, thus receiving the care they need but also actively participating in household decisions and disciplining children because they hold a position of authority in the household (Chan, 1988). Strom and Sato (1995) found that Japanese grandparents derive satisfaction from sharing feelings; advising, counseling, helping, and being with grandchildren; and monitoring the grandchildren's academic performance. They also found that these grandparents want to be effective family members through various positive behaviors: being good listeners, remaining positive, learning from their grandchildren, reinforcing the goals of parents, and accepting help from their grandchildren.

Al Awad and Sonuga-Barke (1992) found that African family group norms consist of communal interdependence, intergenerational harmony, and social conformity. Their findings show that Sudanese children who are brought up in traditional extended families fare better than those in nuclear families. They also note that the role of the grandmother has important functions: to provide advice and information; educate and instruct about cultural practices and conduct; provide social support to increase parent efficacy; provide security and discipline; and take over the mother's role when there is a newborn child. African values of communalism and patriarchy were reconfigured with the arrival of Africans on American soil. Even the experience of slavery did not completely disrupt these established cultural traditions (Billingsley, 1968; Nobles, 1978, 1981). This new structure built on the traditions of kin and nonkin relationships and the elasticity of family boundaries (Scott-Jones & Nelson-LeGall, 1986; Stack, 1974), which built interdependent networks of support and assistance (Wilson, 1991) for African American families.

Woods (1996) found more similarities than differences among Native American, Japanese, and African family structures where the stress is on communal and collective roles and responsibilities, interdependent kinship networks, and maintenance of the culture—which includes history, traditions, cultural practices, and acceptable behavior and conduct. While all three carry obligatory responsibilities by all family members, the level of obligation is higher in Japanese families.

Immigrant families have been found to employ several adaptive strategies: family extendedness and role flexibility, biculturalism, and teaching ancestral views (Harrison, Wilson, Pine, Chan, & Buriel, 1990). For Asian Indians, the patriarchal joint family system is the primary source of socialization of young children (Roopnarine & Hossain, 1992), where the importance of familial bonds, strong religious beliefs, and familial solidarity is incorporated into parenting practices. Family extendedness and role flexibility are manifested differently for immigrant mothers, who live in multigenerational households where they exhibit lower empathetic awareness of children's needs for several reasons. Since they are taking care of elderly parents, the expectation is that their children will take care of them, especially in adapting to bicultural behaviors and language usage. Also, because of the large support network of child care within the family, immigrant mothers tend to be less aware of the needs of their children and less responsive to fulfilling those needs (Jambunathan, Burts, & Pierce, 2000). This unresponsiveness should not be seen as a deficit in parenting practices, though, since it has been established that extended family contexts provide children with a variety of support mechanisms not available to nuclear families.

While investigating the role of grandparents in imparting knowledge and wisdom to young children, Woods (1996) found that in each of the three cultures—Native American, Japanese, and African—grandparents assume positions of authority. While Native American grandmothers provide active parenting in teaching responsibility and discipline, the grandfathers perpetuate tribal history through storytelling. African grandmothers, similarly, engage in active parenting to build socialization processes and to conform to family life. African grandmothers also serve as substitute parents for new mothers. Japanese grandmothers, though, provide a somewhat different role through their instruction in manners, morals, expectations, and discipline.

The most important attributes of families, therefore, are close, involved, and positive relationships with a rich variety of family members, extended family, and nonkin support networks within the neighborhood and community. As a society, we need to understand and appreciate the dimensions and variety of family groupings that provide children with warm, supportive environments in which to flourish. We also need to understand that the configuration of the family structure is not as important as the characteristics of that structure. In the classroom, we need to know which parenting style is most appropriate for which child. This can then be translated into an appropriate behavior management practice. For teachers to know what these effective parenting styles and their corresponding behavior management approaches might be, it is extremely important to maintain frequent and effective contact with parents, extended family members, and nonkin who may be part of the children's support networks in the community.

SUPPORTIVE PARENTAL PRACTICES

Darling and Steinberg (1993) distinguish between parenting styles and parenting practices (parenting style defined as a stable complex of attitudes and beliefs that form the context in which parenting behaviors occur; parenting practices defined as specific goal-oriented behaviors through which parents perform their parental duties). Parenting practices have a direct effect on children's behavior and outcomes. Brenner and Fox (1999) found that parenting practices aggregate in clusters; they noted a correlation between clusters of maternal parenting practices and parenting styles, thus indicating that parenting styles act as a guide to the types of parenting practices adapted by parents. In a study done with Hispanic parents of high-achieving students, thirty-six supportive parental behaviors were found (Lara-Alecio, Irby, & Ebener, 1997). These behaviors fell into three broad categories: high expectations, belief in education, and home/school link:

Belief in Education
Emphasizes importance of reading
Reads with or to children
Conducts storytelling sessions

Provides problems for solving
Acts as encourager
Demonstrates a caring attitude
Structures time
Establishes limits
Provides feedback
Reinforces successes through intangible/tangible rewards
Teaches child to write
Monitors television viewing
Teaches interpersonal and social skills
Teaches good manners and respect
Assists with math and other projects
Provides books, arts, crafts materials
Exposes children to different learning experiences
Provides emotional support during personal dilemma
Allows children to explore consequences of actions
Allows children to make choices
Restricts leisure time activity for misbehavior

High Expectations
Sets high expectations in the completion of school
Connects education with success
Expresses desire and acts to further own education
Saves money for children's education
Acts as a role model in acquiring an education

Home/School Link
Stays informed about child's education
Solicits information about school from children
Participates in school and school-related activities
Takes leadership roles in school organizations
Volunteers in classrooms
Meets teachers early in the school year
Helps in solving problems at school with children
Attends parent/teacher conferences
Interacts with child on day at school

(Lara-Alecio et al., 1997)

Teachers can utilize this list by finding out what each parent's beliefs and expectations are regarding his or her child's education. Frequent contact with parents can reassure them that you have established appropriate, consistent, and effective control and discipline for their children and that their parenting style is being supported and extended in the classroom.

Horton-Parker (1998) recommends the following strategies, drawn from popular parent training approaches that foster authoritative parenting styles.

> **Empathetic listening**: Parents demonstrate care and responsiveness to children's needs as well as model this behavior to help children learn to be empathetic.
> **Setting limits**: By applying firm discipline in ways that convey caring, behavioral limits can be set for children.
> **Giving choices**: By giving children choices, they are able to assume responsibility and learn that choices have consequences.
> **Confronting misbehavior**: By taking kind, firm action, parents can follow through on rules to control misbehavior.
> **Using logical consequences**: Logical consequences must be directly related to the child's behavior, respectful to the child, and reasonable for both child and parent.
> **Using time-out**: When returning from a time-out, children should be given caring messages.
> **Conveying love**: Parents should always let children know that they are loved and valued in order for them to develop self-esteem.
> **Modeling**: Children are more likely to demonstrate altruistic behaviors if they are modeled. The inverse is true (e.g., aggressive, violent behaviors being modeled on television and computer games).
> **Induction**: By explaining the consequences of actions and finding ways to change these actions through interpersonal dilemmas, parents can help children learn how and why their behaviors are inappropriate and what behavior might be used in place.
> **Didactic instruction**: When parents verbalize reasons for being altruistic or caring, children are much more easily able to understand the importance of prosocial behavior.
> **Assignment of responsibility for tasks**: When children assist others, they think of themselves as helpful people, they learn about others' perspectives and feelings, develop a repertoire of prosocial behaviors, and experience positive reinforcement through parental approval. (Horton-Parker, 1998)

It should be kept in mind that while these authoritative parenting styles are considered positive and desirable in parents of mainstream culture, these characteristics would not necessarily prove successful for children from other cultures. This list of authoritative parenting approaches can also be effectively utilized in the classroom through thoughtful and appropriate use with children from various cultural backgrounds.

The National Education Goals Panel (1995) has called for schools and communities to create a desirable context for teaching and learning in which parents are actively involved in the education of their children through the development of partnerships to increase parental involvement and participation in promoting the social, emotional, and academic growth of their children. Therefore, it is both wise and necessary that teachers and principals develop effective ways to communicate with parents and to support their parenting styles and practices in the classroom.

Yet there are limitations to relying only on family indicators to produce positive social behavior. Families and parenting styles and practices are only one leg of the stool. Still to be considered are spirituality and community.

REFERENCES

Abbott, D. A., Zheng, F. M., & Meredith, W. H. (1992). An evolving definition of the fatherhood role in the People's Republic of China. *International Journal of Sociology of the Family, 22,* 45–54.

Al Awad, A. M. E.-H., & Sonuga-Barke, E. J. S. (1992). Childhood problems in a Sudanese city: A comparison of extended and nuclear families. *Child Development, 63,* 906–914.

Alvirez, D., & Bean, R. (1976). The Mexican-American family. In C. Mindel & R. Havenstein (Eds.), *Ethnic families in America: Patterns and variations* (pp. 271–291). New York: Elsevier.

Baca Zinn, M. (1982). Familism among Chicanos: A theoretical review. *Humbolt Journal of Social Relations, 10,* 224–238.

Baca Zinn, M. (1994). Adaptation and continuity in Mexican-origin families. In R. L. Taylor (Ed.), *Minority families in the United States* (pp. 64–81). Englewood Cliffs, NJ: Prentice Hall.

Bartz, K. W., & Levine, E. S. (1978). Childrearing in black parents: A description and comparison to mainstream and Chicano parents. *Journal of Marriage and the Family, 40,* 709–719.

Baumrind, D. (1966). Effects of authoritative parental control on child behavior. *Child Development, 37,* 887–907.

Baumrind, D. (1971). Current patterns of parental authority. *Developmental Psychology Monographs, 4,* 1–103.

Baumrind, D. (1991). Parenting style and adolescent development. In J. Brooks-Gunn, R. Lerner, and A. C. Peterse (Eds.), *The encyclopedia of adolescence* (pp. 746–758). New York: Garland.

Billingsley, A. (1968). *Black families in white America.* Englewood Cliffs, NJ: Prentice Hall.

Brenner, V., & Fox, R. A. (1999). An empirically derived classification of parenting practices. *Journal of Genetic Psychology, 160,* 343–356.

Carrasquillo, H. (1994). The Puerto Rican family. In R. L. Taylor (Ed.), *Minority families in the United States* (pp. 82–94). Englewood Cliffs, NJ: Prentice Hall.

Chan, F. (1988). To be old and Asian: An unsettling life in America. *Aging, 358,* 14–15.

Darling, N., & Steinberg, L. (1993). Parenting styles as context: An integrative model. *Psychological Bulletin, 113,* 487–496.

Demo, D. H. (2000). Children's experience of family diversity. *National Forum, 80,* 16–20.

Escovar, P. L., & Lazarus, P. J. (1982). Cross-cultural child-rearing practices: Implications for school psychology. *School Psychology International, 3,* 143–148.

Fagan, J. (2000). African American and Puerto Rican American parenting styles, paternal involvement, and Head Start children's social competence. *Merrill-Palmer Quarterly, 46,* 592–612.

Haapasalo, J., & Tremblay, R. E. (1994). Physically aggressive boys from ages 6 to 12: Family background, parenting behavior, and prediction of delinquency. *Journal of Consulting and Clinical Psychology, 62,* 1044–1052.

Harrison, A. O., Wilson, M. N., Pine, C. J., Chan, S. Q., & Buriel, B. (1990). Family ecologies of ethnic minority children. *Child Development, 61,* 347–362.

Hart, C. H., Olsen, S. F., Robinson, C. C., & Mandleco, B. L. (1997). The development of social communicative competence in childhood: Review and a model of person, familial, and extra-familial processes. *Communication Yearbook, 20,* 305–312.

Horejsi, C., Craig, B., & Pablo, J. (1992). Reactions by Native American parents to child protection agencies: Cultural and community factors. *Child Welfare, 71,* 329–342.

Horton-Parker, R. J. (1998). Teaching children to care: Engendering prosocial behavior through humanistic parenting. *Journal of Humanistic Counseling, Education, and Development, 37,* 66–77.

Hutter, M. (1988). *The changing family: Comparative perspectives* (2nd ed.). New York: Macmillan.

Jambunathan, S., Burts, D. C., & Pierce, S. (2000). Comparisons of parenting attitudes among five ethnic groups in the United States. *Journal of Comparative Family Studies, 31,* 395–406.

Kakar, S. (1978). *The inner worlds: A psychoanalytic study of childhood and society in India.* New Delhi: Oxford University Press.

Kohlberg, L., & Candee, D. (1984). The relationship of moral judgment to moral action. In W. M. Kurtines & J. L. Gewirtz (Eds.), *Morality, moral behavior, and moral development* (pp. 53–73). New York: Wiley.

Lara-Alecio, R., Irby, B. J., & Ebener, R. (1997). Developing academically supportive behaviors among Hispanic parents: What elementary teachers and administrators can do. *Preventing School Failure, 42,* 27–32.

Lindahl, K. M., & Malik, N. M. (1999). Marital conflict, family processes, and boys' externalizing behavior in Hispanic American and European American families. *Journal of Clinical Child Psychology, 28,* 12–24.

Maccoby, E. E., & Martin, J. A. (1983). Socialization in the context of the family: Parent-child interaction. In P. H. Mussen (Series Ed.) & E. M Hetherington (Vol. Ed.), *Handbook of child psychology: Vol. 4. Socialization, personality, and social development* (4th ed., pp. 1–101). New York: Wiley.

McAdoo, J. L. (1979). A study of father-child interaction patterns and self-esteem in black preschool children. *Young Children, 34,* 46–53.

McAdoo, J. L. (1981). Black father and child interaction. In L. Gary (Ed.), *Black men.* Beverly Hills, CA: Sage.

Mirande, A. (1979). A reinterpretation of male dominance in the Chicano family. *The Family Coordinator, 28,* 473–479.

Mirande, A. (1985). *The Chicano experience.* Notre Dame, IN: University of Notre Dame Press.

National Education Goals Panel. (1995). *Building a nation of learners.* Washington, D.C.: U.S. Government Printing Office.

Nobles, W. (1978). Toward an empirical and theoretical framework for defining black families. *Journal of Marriage and the Family, 430,* 679–688.

Nobles, W. (1981). African-American family life: An instrument of culture. In H. P. McAdoo (Ed.), *Black families* (pp. 77–86). Newbury Park, CA: Sage.

Quoss, B., & Wen, Z. (1995). Parenting styles and children's satisfaction with parenting in China and the United States. *Journal of Comparative Family Studies, 26,* 265–280.

Rashid, H. (1985). Black family research and parent education programs: The need for convergence. *Contemporary Education, 56,* 180–185.

Roopnarine, J. L., & Hossain, Z. (1992). Parent–child interactions in urban Indian families: Are they changing? In J. L. Roopnarine & D. B. Carter (Eds.), *Annual advances in applied psychology* (pp. 1–17). New Jersey: Ablex Publishing Corporation.

Ross, A. D. (1967). *The Hindu family in the urban setting.* Toronto: University of Toronto Press.

Rubin, K. H., Stewart, S. L., & Chen, X. (1994). Parents of aggressive and withdrawn children. In M. Bornstein (Ed.), *Handbook of parenting, Vol. 1* (pp. 255–284). Hillsdale, NJ: Erlbaum.

Russell, A., Aloa, V., Feder, T., Glover, A., Miller, H., & Palmer, G. (1998). Sex-based differences in parenting styles in a sample with preschool children. *Australian Journal of Psychology, 50,* 1–11.

Scott-Jones, D., & Nelson-LeGall, S. (1986). Defining black families: Past and present. In E. Seidman & J. Pappaport (Eds.), *Redefining social problems* (pp. 83–100). New York: Plenum.

Shek, T. L. (2000). Differences between fathers and mothers in the treatment of, and relationship with, their teenage children: Perceptions of Chinese adolescents. *Adolescence, 35,* 135–146.

Smetana, J. G. (1995). Parenting styles and conceptions of parental authority during adolescence. *Child Development, 66,* 299–316.

Stack, C. B. (1974). *All our kin: Strategies for survival in a black community.* New York: Harper & Row.

Steinberg, L., Lamborn, S. D., Darling, N., Mounts, N. S., & Dronbusch, S. M. (1994). Over-time changes in adjustment and competence among adolescents from authoritative, authoritarian, indulgent, and neglectful families. *Child Development, 65,* 754–770.

Strom, R., & Sato, S. (1995). Grandparents in Japan: A three-generational study. *International Journal of Aging and Human Development, 40,* 209–226.

Taylor, R. J., Chatters, L. M., Tucker, M. B., & Lewis, E. (1990). Developments in research on black families: A decade review. *Journal of Marriage and the Family, 52,* 993–1014.

Vargas, M. (1991). Predictors of maternal teaching strategies in Puerto Rican mothers. Unpublished doctoral dissertation, Fordham University, Bronx, New York.

Wasserman, G. A., Miller, L. S., Pinner, E., & Jaramillo, B. (1996). Parenting predictors of early conduct problems in urban, high-risk boys. *Journal of American Academy of Child Adolescent Psychiatry, 35,* 1227–1236.

Wilson, M. N. (1991). The context of the African-American family. In J. Everett, S. Chipungu, & B. Leashore (Eds.), *Child welfare: An Afrocentric perspective* (pp. 85–118). Princeton, NJ: Rutgers University Press.

Woods, R. D. (1996). Grandmother roles: A cross-cultural view. *Journal of Instructional Psychology, 23,* 286–293.

Youniss, J., & Smollar, J. (1985). *Adolescent relations with mothers, fathers, and friends.* Chicago: University of Chicago Press.

CHAPTER 3

Religion and Spirituality

Just as parenting styles differ across cultures, so does the use of religion and spirituality in setting codes of conduct and in instilling moral and ethical values. To examine the role of religion in setting standards for nonviolent behavior, it is necessary to consider several questions.

- How can knowledge of the hard and soft aspects of religions advance our understanding of violence?
- What is religion's role in society?
- What is the God image, and what role does it play in setting values?
- How do parents' religious beliefs impact children's belief systems?
- What are the relationships between religious beliefs, parenting styles, and value orientations?

RELIGION: HARD AND SOFT ASPECTS

In an effort to provide structure to the religious landscape, Galtung (1997) placed religions into three broad segments: Occidental religions, Hindu religions, and Oriental religions. These not only represent extremely varied religious experiences but also offer geographical logic in their variance.

> As we move eastward God dies somewhere between Hinduism and Buddhism. Before that, between Islam and Hinduism, Satan has already perished. Faith loosens up. Rather than the occidental either-or, this faith or that, there is an Oriental both-and, this faith and that one. And

the faith(s) chosen or grown into are no longer seen as universally valid; validity for me/us does not imply validity for all. The individual soul is de-emphasized, from a knot of individual ownership in this life, via shared ownership with others in a series of reincarnations, to a vague dispersal of the ego into the net with others, the sum total of all relations with other beings, past, present and future. Life goals change dramatically: from the eternal continuation of individual existence, next to God, to transcendence to a higher existence devoid of individual and permanent identity, [sic] Nibbana. (Galtung, 1997)

In viewing this broad spectrum of religions for inclinations toward condoning or rejecting violence, Galtung (1997) found that Buddhism clearly rejects both structural violence (i.e., violence built into social structures) and direct violence (i.e., violence by the individual). Embedded in Buddhist doctrine are two aspects that foment the rejection of violence: nonviolence, or ahimsa, and nonpossession, or avoidance of having too much. Hinduism shares the doctrine of ahimsa but accepts a major form of structural violence, the caste system. While Islam rejects caste, it accepts other forms of both structural and direct violence to defend the faith through just wars, or jihads.[1] Christianity and Judaism are weak in both dimensions, condoning violence or not having clear and explicit doctrines against it. It is therefore interesting to note that Judaism, Christianity, and Islam, the three religions that believe in singularism (i.e., the validity of only one faith) and universalism (i.e., the validity of the one faith for the whole world) (Galtung, 1997) are currently involved in the use of force and terror against other governments. The use of force by the Americans to drive out the Taliban from Afghanistan, the use of terror by the Palestinians to disrupt the economies of the United States and Israel, and the use of force by the Israelis—the Chosen People—to rout out the terrorists are all embedded in the religious belief systems of these countries.

More than just the hardness of the Occidental religions and the softness of those in the East is the hard-to-soft continuum within each religion. Examples of this include the orthodox–conservative–reformed triad in Judaism or the various denominations in Christianity, where the continuum goes from conservative churches—Baptist, Pentecostal (Assembly of God and Church of God), Jehovah's Witnesses, Mormon, Church of

Christ, Nazarene, Seventh Day Adventist—to moderate churches—Lutheran, Disciples of Christ, and Catholic—to liberal churches—Methodist, Presbyterian, Episcopalian, and United Church of Christ (Perrin, 1989). But even within each denomination, hard and soft elements exist, ranging from fundamentalist ideologies to liberation theological principles. At times, there is more similarity among hard aspects (fundamentalism) or soft aspects (liberalism) of the various religions than perhaps there might be within the denomination itself. Therefore, while many religions can perpetuate violence, they also have in their doctrines the capacity to construct peace and nonviolence.

RELIGION'S ROLE IN SOCIETY

It has been well documented that religion enhances individual quality of life. The integrative and regulative nature of closely knit religious communities, the structure of religious communities, and how such structures may enhance the welfare of individual community members has been studied thoroughly (Ellison, 1994; Ellison & George, 1994; Welch, Tittle, & Petee, 1991). The positive effects of religious beliefs and religious worldviews on well-being have also been the center of much research (Berger, 1967; Ellison, Gay, & Glass, 1989; Pollner, 1989; Pargament et al., 1990; Williams, 1994). Furthermore, Ellison and George (1994), Ellison (1994), and Welch, Tittle, and Petee (1991) found that frequent churchgoers report larger social networks, more contacts with network members, more types of social support received, and more favorable perceptions of their social relationships. They also found that the moral constraints of religious communities regulate and constrain behavior in ways that facilitate good physical health, positive family and interpersonal relations, ethical work conduct and financial dealings, and the inhibition of stress-inducing lifestyles (Bjarnason, 1998).

Another important aspect of religion's role in society is the primacy of horizontal religion over vertical religion (Lenksi, 1961). In this study, Lenksi found that the level of participation in one's church for worship-related and extra-religious purposes (horizontal religion) was a stronger predictor of other social behavior and values than religious belief (vertical religion) itself (Lenski, 1961).

This protective capacity to enhance life, though, has its weak spot in the Western religions where benefits are only dispensed to each denomination's believers. In the either-or type of faith (i.e., my God or yours), the potential for conflict is greater, whether it be on an individual basis or on a grander scale as seen in the current tensions as well as in the centuries of wars waged in the name of religion.

GOD IMAGES

God images are another important aspect of religion and spirituality for educators to study because parents' images of God are reflected in their children's impressions of parenting styles, which in turn predict children's images of God (Hertel & Donahue, 1995).

God has variously been seen in the dimensions of judging–nurturing, controlling–saving, and concrete–abstract (Krejci 1994; Krejci, Erickson, & Aune 1992; Krejci, Jette, & Anderson, 1993). In conducting research on individuals' internal constructions of God through use of concept mapping, Kunkel, Cook, Meshel, Daughtry, and Hauerstein (1999) found a wide variation of God images along the dimensions of punitive versus nurturant and mystical versus anthropomorphic. The study found distinct regions of God images. Human images of God tended to be grouped by role and regulating functions. Other God image groupings were powerful, benevolent, inspirational, mysterious, and vengeful. Nurturant images of God (e.g., creator, everlasting, and everywhere) were more prevalent than punitive images (e.g., intimidating and unfair), while mystical and anthropomorphic images of God were about equal (Kunkel et al., 1999). These findings further support earlier findings that Americans emphasize supportive images of God and that God is seen more in terms of love than authority (Nelson, Cheek, & Au, 1985; Hertel & Donahue, 1995).

While these studies provide a good sense of essentially how Christian parents and children develop concepts of God, they leave unanswered how other religions, theistic and atheistic, would respond to these or similar prompts. Taking Spiro's view (1996) of religion as an institution consisting of culturally patterned interaction with culturally postulated superhuman beings, Buddhism, while regarded by some as atheistic, has

Buddha as its superhuman being who acquired the power to attain enlightenment and showed others how to attain it (Orru & Wang, 1992). Therefore, much more research needs to be done to give educators a sense of how to work with children who come from non-Christian backgrounds. What importance, then, do these findings have in regard to setting codes of conduct and instilling moral and ethical principles in children?

IMPACT OF PARENTS' RELIGIOUS BELIEFS ON CHILDREN'S BELIEF SYSTEMS

In a study done by Dickie and Eshleman (1997) on parent–child relationships and children's images of God, several factors were revealed regarding children's perceptions of God, mothers, and fathers. Two groups were studied, one from mainline Protestant upper middle class and the other from diverse inner-city backgrounds. Regarding children's perceptions of God as being the same or different from their mothers or fathers, it was found that all younger children perceived God as different from mother and father and that mother was more different from God than father. Older children from mainline backgrounds perceived God to be more like mother than father, but older children from diverse inner-city backgrounds found God, mother, and father equally similar. Mainline girls also found God more similar to both parents, while diverse girls found God not like their parents.

Regarding children's perceptions of whether or not God, mothers, and/or fathers were nurturing, the study found that all young children from both groups perceived authority figures to be less nurturing, while all older children from both groups perceived God to be nurturing. Regarding children's perceptions of whether or not God, mothers, and/or fathers were powerful, the study found that young mainline boys perceived God, father, and mother as powerful, while young mainline girls perceived mother more powerful than God or father. Older diverse girls found God, mother, and father equally powerful, while diverse boys and girls found father to be more powerful than mother. Dickie and Eshleman (1997) also found that gender experiences shape children's perceptions of authority (Gilligan & Attanuaci, 1988; Gilligan & Wiggins, 1988; Chodorow, 1978), where the diverse group held more traditional gender-role views: mother as more nurturing than father. Finally, this study showed that father's nurturance was the best predictor of God's nurturance, and mother's power was the best predictor of God's power.

In the same area of research, Hertel and Donahue (1995) found that girls more than boys viewed God as love, while boys more often viewed God as authoritarian. The same gender differences appeared in parents as well. Nelsen, Potvin, and Shields (1977) and Hertel and Donahue found that children see parents more as sources of love than of authority, and both boys and girls viewed mothers as more loving than fathers. Also found in the same study was that when parents viewed God as loving, then the children had a greater tendency to view parents as loving. Furthermore, it was found that mothers were more dominant in the religious socialization of their children and therefore, in their role as disciplinarian, influenced their children's images of God more than fathers did.

All of what has been reported thus far has been in the context of Western religious thought and practice. Therefore, these data are useful only in that context. These studies do not shed light on how children and parents who practice non-Western religions would view representations of the supernatural and transcendental and how that would, in turn, affect children's religious belief systems. Much more research needs to be done to include non-Western religious traditions as they relate to the way parents' religious beliefs impact their children's religious beliefs.

RELATIONSHIP BETWEEN RELIGIOUS BELIEFS, VALUE ORIENTATIONS, AND PARENTING STYLES

As shown in the previous chapter, the efficacy of authoritative parenting style in mainstream families results in positive behavior outcomes such as increased competence, autonomy, and self-esteem; better problem-solving skills, academic performance, and peer relations; more self-reliance; and less deviance or aggressive behavior (Steinberg, Lamborn, Darling, Mounts, & Dronbusch, 1994). Yet authoritarian parenting, which is ineffective in mainstream families, is used extensively in Hispanic families. In the Hispanic family context, authoritarian parenting is successful since it is tempered with interdependence, nurturance, responsiveness, and consistency, thus providing the same sort of support structures as seen in mainstream family authoritative parenting (Alvirez & Bean, 1976; Baca Zinn, 1982; Carrasquillo, 1994; Mirande, 1979, 1985). African American parents have also been found to use a strict parenting style where a great deal of emphasis is placed on respect for authority, yet they also display high levels of support and expression of emotions (Bartz & Levine, 1978; Rashid, 1985; Taylor, Chatters, Tucker, & Lewis, 1990).

Studies linking parental religious beliefs and child rearing have found that some fundamentalist religious beliefs likely encourage more authoritarian norms of parenting (Dobson, 1976; Meier, 1977) and that contemporary fundamentalist literature on parenting stresses the certainty and legitimacy of biblical texts that emphasize obedience and submission to authority (Peshkin, 1986; Rose, 1988). In following these threads, Danso, Hunsberger, and Pratt (1997) began to look at the relationships among and between right-wing authoritarianism and religious fundamentalism, obedience, faithkeeping, and acceptance of corporal punishment to ascertain the effects these valuing positions would have on child behavior outcomes and child autonomy.

Altemeyer (1981) defines right-wing authoritarianism as *authoritarian submission*, a high degree of submission to the authorities who are perceived to be established and legitimate in the society in which one lives; *authoritarian aggression* as a general aggressiveness, directed against various persons, which is perceived to be sanctioned by established authorities; and *conventionalism* as a high degree of adherence to the social conventions perceived to be endorsed by society and its established authorities.

Danso et al. (1997) found that the right-wing authoritarian disposition of parents is importantly related to their self-reported parenting styles. It can be seen from figure 3.1 that right-wing authoritarianism drives the religious fundamental beliefs, which are then connected to faithkeeping, obedience, and acceptance of corporal punishment. Religiosity is not necessarily an important predictor of parents' child-rearing beliefs, but it does become important when mediated by right-wing authoritarian beliefs.

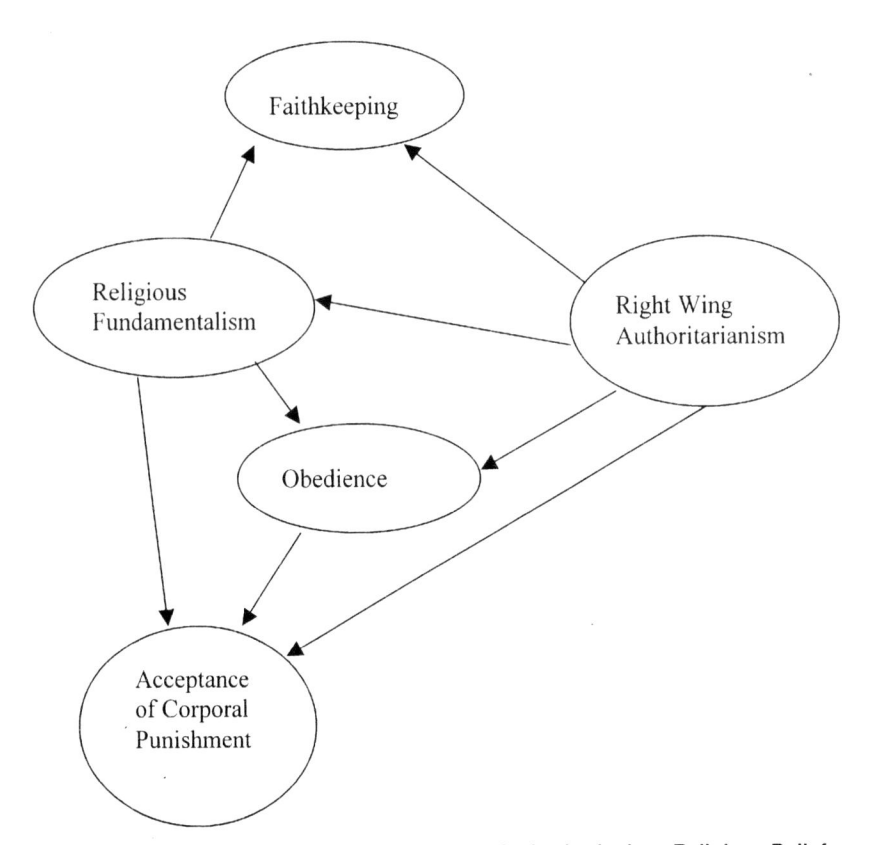

Figure 3.1. Relationships Among Right-Wing Authoritarianism, Religious Beliefs, and Parenting Styles

All of these factors—right-wing authoritarianism, religious fundamentalism, obedience, faithkeeping, and acceptance of corporal punishment—were all negatively related to child autonomy for both parents (Danso et al.).

Therefore, in summarizing the data on the role of religion and spirituality in developing children who are nonviolent, it can be seen that religion has the potential to provide the support, nurturing, and community that children need. But it is also evident that right-wing authoritarian beliefs mediate the normal nurturing and supportive system that religion affords and thus create homes where authoritarian parenting styles are prevalent. While this might be effective with Hispanic and African American children, it has been shown that authoritarian parenting styles are destructive to mainstream children. This has enormous implications for half of our population and might help explain the violence that has taken place in the essentially white heartland of America.

Obviously, more research needs to be done with children from various cultures and ethnicities to see how these elements fall together and to trace how patterns of authoritarian beliefs, religious beliefs, and parenting styles create certain conditions for children to develop proclivities for violence or nonviolence.

NOTE

1. Jihad is meant to be exertion of the faith: an internal struggle of self to become as ethically and morally sound as possible. The word has been corrupted by certain extremist elements in Islam to mean use of violence to defend the faith through holy war.

REFERENCES

Altemeyer, H. (1981). *Right-wing authoritarianism.* Winnipeg: University of Manitoba Press.

Alvirez, D., & Bean, R. (1976). Ethnic families in America: Patterns and variations. In C. Mindel and R. Havenstein (Eds.), *The Mexican-American family* (pp. 271–291). New York: Elsevier.

Baca Zinn, M. (1982). Familism among Chicanos: A theoretical review. *Humbolt Journal of Social Relations, 10,* 224–238.

Bartz, K. W., & Levine, E. S. (1978). Child rearing in black parents: A description and comparison to Anglo and Chicano parents. *Journal of Marriage and the Family, 40,* 709–719.

Berger, P. (1967). *The sacred canopy: Elements of sociological theory of religion.* New York: Doubleday.

Bjarnason, T. (1998). Parents, religion and perceived social coherence: A Durkheimian framework of adolescent anomie. *Journal for the Scientific Study of Religion, 37,* 742–755.

Carrasquillo, H. (1994). The Puerto Rican family. In R. L. Taylor (Ed.), *Minority families in the United States* (pp. 82–94). Englewood Cliffs, NJ: Prentice Hall.

Chodorow, N. (1978). *The reproduction of mothering: Psychoanalysis and the sociology of gender.* Los Angeles: University of California Press.

Danso, H., Hunsberger, B., & Pratt, M. (1997). The role of parental religious fundamentalism and right-wing authoritarianism in child rearing: Goals and practices. *Journal for the Scientific Study of Religion, 36,* 496–512.

Dickie, J. R., & Eshleman, A. K. (1997). Parent–child relationships and children's images of God. *Journal for the Scientific Study of Religion, 36,* 25–44.

Dobson, J. (1976). *The strong-willed child: Birth through adolescence.* Wheaton, IL: Living Books/Tyndale House.

Ellison, C. G. (1994). Religion, the life stress paradigm, and the study of depression. In J. S. Levin (Ed.), *Religion in aging and health: Theoretical foundations and methodological frontiers* (pp. 78–121). Thousand Oaks, CA: Sage.

Ellison, C. G., Gay, D. A., & Glass, T. A. (1989). Does religious commitment contribute to individual life satisfaction? *Social Forces, 68,* 100–123.

Ellison, C. G., & George, L. K. (1994). Religious involvement, social ties and social support in a Southeastern community. *Journal for the Scientific Study of Religion, 33,* 46–61.

Galtung, J. (1997). Religions, hard and soft. *Cross Currents, 47* (4), 437–451.

Gilligan, C., & Attanuaci, J. T. (1988). Two moral orientations. In C. Gilligan, J. V. Ward, & J. M. Taylor (Eds.), *Mapping the moral domain.* Cambridge: Harvard University Press.

Gilligan C., & Wiggins, G. (1988). The origins of morality in early childhood relationships. In C. Gilligan, J. V. Ward, & J. M. Taylor (Eds.), *Mapping the moral domain.* Cambridge: Harvard University Press.

Hertel, B. R., & Donahue, M. J. (1995). Parental influences on God images among children: Testing Durkheim's metaphoric parallelism. *Journal for the Scientific Study of Religion, 34,* 186–200.

Krejci, M. J. (1994). Gender comparison of God images via multidimensional scaling analysis. In M. A. Kunkel (Chair), Approaches to uncovering the latent structure of religious concepts. Symposium presented at the annual meeting of the American Psychological Association, Los Angeles.

Krejci, M. J., Erickson, L., & Aune, J. E. (1992). *Images of God: A gender comparison via multidimensional scaling analysis.* Paper presented at the annual meeting of the American Psychological Association, Washington, D.C.

Krejci, M. J., Jette, A. M., & Anderson, L. J. (1993). *God image comparison across family developmental stages.* Paper presented at the annual meeting of the Amscan Psychological Association, Toronto, Canada.

Kunkel, M. A., Cook, S., Meshel, D. S., Daughtry, D., & Hauerstein, A. (1999). God images: A concept map. *Journal for the Scientific Study of Religion, 38,* 193–203.

Lenksi, G. (1961). *The religious factor: A sociological study of religion's impact on politics, economics, and family life.* Garden City, NY: Doubleday.

Meier, P. D. (1977). *Christian child rearing and personality development.* Grand Rapids, MI: Baker House.

Mirande, A. (1979). A reinterpretation of male dominance in the Chicano family. *Family Coordinator, 28,* 473–479.

Mirande, A. (1985). *The Chicano experience.* Notre Dame, IN: University of Notre Dame Press.

Nelsen, H. M., Potvin, R. H., & Shields, J. (1977). *The religion of children.* Washington, D.C.: United States Catholic Conference.

Nelson, H. M., Cheek, N. H., & Au, P. (1985). Gender difference in images of God. *Journal for the Scientific Study of Religion, 24,* 396–402.

Nelson, H. M., Potvin, R. H., & Shields, J. (1977). *The religion of children.* Washington, D.C.: United States Catholic Conference.

Orru, M., & Wang, A. (1992). Durkheim, religion, and Buddhism. *Journal for the Scientific Study of Religion, 31,* 47–62.

Pargament, K. I., Ensing, D. S., Falgout, K., Olsen, H., Reilly, B., Van Haitsma, K., & Warren, R. (1990). God help me: Religious coping efforts as predictors of the outcomes of significant negative life events. *American Journal of Community Psychology, 18,* 793–824.

Peshkin, A. (1986). *God's choice: The total world of a fundamentalist Christian school.* Chicago: University of Chicago Press.

Perrin, R. D. (1989). American religion in the post-Aquarian age: Values and demographic factors in church growth and decline. *Journal for the Scientific Study of Religion, 28,* 75–89.

Pollner, M. (1989). Divine relations, social relations, and well-being. *Journal of Health and Social Behavior, 30,* 92–104.

Rashid, H. (1985). Black family research and parent education programs: The need for convergence. *Contemporary Education, 56,* 180–185.

Rose, S. D. (1988). *Keeping them out of the hands of Satan: Evangelical schooling in America.* New York: Routledge, Chapman, and Hall.

Spiro, M. E. (1996). Religion: Problems of definition and explanation. In M. Banton (Ed.), *Anthropological approaches to the study of religion* (pp. 85–126). New York: Praeger.

Steinberg, L., Lamborn, S. D., Darling, N., Mounts, N. S., & Dronbusch, S. M. (1994). Over-time changes in adjustment and competence among adolescents from authoritative, authoritarian, indulgent, and neglectful families. *Child Development, 65,* 754–770.

Taylor, R. J., Chatters, L. M., Tucker, M. B., & Lewis, E. (1990). Developments in research on black families: A decade review. *Journal of Marriage and the Family, 52,* 993–1014.

Welch, M. R., Tittle, C. R., & Petee, T. (1991). Religion and deviance among adult Catholics: A test of the "moral communities" hypothesis. *Journal of the Scientific Study of Religion, 30,* 159–172.

Williams, D. R. (1994). The measurement of religion in epidemiologic studies: Problems and prospects. In J. S. Levin (Ed.), *Religion in aging and health: Theoretical foundations and methodological frontiers* (pp. 125–148). Thousand Oaks, CA: Sage.

CHAPTER 4

Community

For teachers to find effective ways of working with their students and reducing violence in classrooms and schools, it is necessary to thoroughly know the context of the community in which they work. Important aspects include the fundamental characteristics of the community, the levels of social agency available in the community, strategies that are in place to develop social capital within the community, mediating circumstances that inhibit and promote community building, and the goals the community has for its citizens (Chaskin, 2001). Community capacity and available social capital are what will provide the needed support and resources to help educators develop better educational outcomes in classrooms and schools.

CHARACTERISTICS OF COMMUNITY

In examining the characteristics of the community, educators should seek answers to the following questions. Consider these questions in the context of your role as an educator.

- To what degree do people feel connected to one another in the community? To what degree do you see this manifested in your school and classroom?
- To what degree do people trust and support one another and provide access to resources (Coleman, 1988; Putnam, 1993)? To what degree are these qualities apparent in your school and classroom?

- Is there a threshold of collectively held values, norms, and vision (McMillian & Chavis, 1986) that allows for collective action and support of a common good (Crenshaw & St. John, 1989; Guest & Lee, 1983; Suttles, 1972)? How is the diversity of the parents and community members brought together in your schools and classrooms to allow for the various voices to be included in the dialogue and decision making yet provide for collective concerns to be voiced and collective action to be taken?
- Are there individuals, groups, and organizations that are willing to take charge and actively participate in making decisions for the common good? Are they representative of the various constituencies of the community? Are these various constituencies represented in the schools?
- What kinds of resources at both the formal and informal levels are available—economic, human, physical, and political—for the people to draw on inside and outside the neighborhood to address issues of concern (Chaskin, 2001)? What levels and types of resources are you able to draw on in your classroom?
- What kinds of human capital and leadership does the community possess? What levels of skills, knowledge, and resources do individuals possess (Chaskin, 2001)? To what degree do you find these skills, knowledge, and resources available to you in your classroom or school?
- To what degree do community-based organizations function competently and support the development of social capital? How do they incorporate representation of community members, influence the political structure, and engage in interorganizational relationships (Glickman & Servon, 1997)? To what degree is there meaningful representation of the people of the community? What meaningful organizational representation of the community do you find in your school and classroom?
- How does community engagement produce positive effects for the community (e.g., better services, greater influence on public policy decision making, greater residential stability, and development of sustainable community capacity) (Chaskin, 2001)? How does parent and community participation in your school leverage more resources and programs for the children in your classroom?

- How are the following developed in the community: effective leadership and organizations; community mobilization; and fostering of collaboration among individuals, groups, and organizations (Chaskin, 2001)? How are these skills and processes manifested in the schools?
- What goals does the community have for its citizens? What goals does your community have for its schools? Are they realistic, based on the answers to your previous questions? If not, how can the community be mobilized to create the social capital needed to meet these goals?

It is in the community, this larger social context, that each family interacts, integrates, and negotiates each day. Parent–child relationships, spirituality, and other familial contexts are played out on this large social canvas. The school is one of the institutions at the center of this context, where the symptoms of the society are most visible. Are these symptoms healthy or problematic? Are there racial and ethnic conflicts? Is there an unequal distribution of power and wealth? Is there political and religious polarization? What assets does the community already possess that can be the starting point for growing community capacity and social capital?

Social capital includes the "abilities to develop and sustain strong relationships, solve problems and make group decisions, and collaborate effectively to identify goals and get work done" (Mattessich & Monsey, 1997). Building social capital is a spiraling process.

> Progressing up the rungs of the ladder is not a one-way journey. It is necessary to move up and down, engaging in community problem-solving, then using the results to strengthen localized social capital, and then beginning again with the goal of creating a civic culture that supports trust and collaborations. (Potapchuk, Crocker, & Schechter, 1997)

Social capital is the glue that holds a community together. This includes the

> neighbor who knows all the children on the block and can be counted on to be there for them in an emergency or during a conflict. It is also the police officer who lives in the neighborhood and coaches the soccer team

on which the neighbor's daughter plays. It is also the neighborhood association members and the volunteers at the community center and homeless shelter. They are the people who carry forward the values and vision of the community along with the parents, the houses of worship, and the other civic institutions. (Potapchuk, Crocker, & Schechter, 1997)

An effective way to get at the issues raised by the previous questions is to organize responses into a framework that can help teachers develop effective capacity building and social capital, both inside the schools and in the larger community. The framework provides a structure to build community at the level of family, neighborhood, workplace and school, as well as in the larger culture. The framework derives from the work of Bronfenbrenner (1979) and more recently Garbarino (1995), who developed a way of looking at the bridge between family life and the larger society. While the four-tiered schema of the social context, called the micro-, meso-, exo-, and macro-systems (Bronfenbrenner, 1979), is a flexible and dynamic system that cannot be artificially divided into these parts, they are still useful in developing an understanding of how to create social capital and community capacity in the schools and community.

Bronfenbrenner's micro-system is the complex of interrelations within the immediate setting where people interact with one another, the smallest unit being a family. Families come in various forms—nuclear, extended, one parent, extended matriarchal, single-gender parents, and so on. As such, this micro-system is as complex as the individual family unit itself. Within the structure of immediate and extended family, there are various levels of support, interaction, and shared values. If the family demonstrates social responsibility for the health and welfare of all, then social capital and capacity are built at this level. If the family values include principles of social justice, equity, and democracy, then the capital generated by the family can be utilized in the meso-system (neighborhood level) to build more social capital. As a family unit, collaboration consists of participation in Parents as Teachers programs, adult literacy and education, and family activity nights at school.

The meso-system is where the family participates in a larger social context (e.g., neighborhood, school, work, and communities of faith). At this level, families are now engaged in block events, community center activities, and social and cultural organizations. Responsibilities to family and neighborhood expand to include block watches, teachers living in the districts where they teach, neighborhood policing, tenant management, and citizen advisory committees. Their shared values are put into a larger cauldron of values community-wide to work cohesively on participatory neighborhood associations and interfaith organizations. Their collaboration at this level includes after-school tutoring programs, Head Start, networks of lending associations, police–community partnerships, Habitat for Humanity, and soup kitchen participation. Provided they build positive experiences for all, youth league sports—especially those sports that include girls—can potentially provide perfect opportunities for parents to address issues of violence and unacceptable behavior by extending the discussion and resolution of these issues into their own families beyond the playing fields and sports arenas.

The exo-system brings the family into an even larger circle of institutions and markets in which events occur that affect the family's immediate environment. At this level, families interact with business and civic organizations and get help from small business loan agencies and community development banks. The shared vision includes regional workforce development strategies. Collaboration consists of working with incubators for small businesses, school-to-work programs, multisector partnerships, cooperatives, and regional workforce development.

Bronfenbrenner's macro-system is where cultural values and belief systems are brought to bear on the other systems. It is at this level that families participate in state and national political and economic organizations and find help through federal and state grants, foundation grants, and corporate grants. It is where they are at the mercy of the stock markets, national and international crises, wars, and natural disasters, and where shared vision must be modified and molded to the needs of the larger society. Building economic capacity, as a shared vision, is followed by the creation of economic empowerment zones. It is also where the clash of national cultures is to be found, such as the wars in the Middle East where a clash of values and vision creates more chaos rather than solutions and the building of human and physical capital.

As shown in table 4.1, the characteristics of social capital that build community capacity and lead to empowerment are interaction, responsibility, shared vision, and collaboration and inclusion. Interaction involves active participation and communication on issues for the common good. Responsibility is the coalescing of groups through trust and cooperation to invest in their social capital. Shared vision represents the threshold of shared values that lead to agreement on the end product, plus recognition that there will be a variety of processes and procedures to get there. Collaboration and inclusion produce an inclusive atmosphere where resources are pooled to solve problems that are mutually agreed upon. It is at this stage that people feel they have a voice in the problem solving and decision making, as well as direct involvement in the processes that will lead to positive change in the community. Also involved in collaboration is trust, where people deliver on promises and support one another to resolve conflict. This also leads to a sense of belonging and therefore the ability to be an active participant in the building of the community.

While this might appear very easy to do, through the building of social capital from the smallest to the largest units of the social context, it is really fraught with problems. However, this should not deter us from trying. Each community will have its unique list of circumstances and problems it must cope with. There may be large amounts of negative social capital that tear at the fabric of the community (e.g., racial and ethnic conflict, religious and political polarization, unequal distribution of wealth and power). There may also be street gangs, gated communities, militia groups, and supremacist groups on the right and on the left. While these groups have high levels of social capital because of their cohesiveness, shared values, and collaboration, they do not contribute to the building of a strong, nonviolent civil society. Garbarino (1995) identified socially toxic communities in a Western context that were materially impoverished yet were not poor in social capital, explaining that social class is not necessarily a given regarding lack of social capital. It is possible for a lower income neighborhood to hold high social capital, or an upper income neighborhood could be bankrupt of social capital. So what is a healthy community? It is one with sufficient economic support not to be at risk, including low-income neighborhoods that are high in cohesive social capital.

Table 4.1. Building Community Capacity

Characteristics of Social Capital	Immediate and Extended Families	Neighborhood, Communities of Faith, School, Work	Institutions, Markets	Societal Culture
Interaction	Family reunions, family travel and activities	Block events, community centers, social and cultural organizations, youth league sports	Business and civic organizations	State and national economic and political organizations and government
Responsibility	Family support for children's health, education, and welfare	Block watches, teachers living in districts where they teach, neighborhood policing, tenant management teams, citizen advisory committees	Small business loan agencies, local government block grants, community development banks	Federal and state government grants, foundation grants, corporate grants
Shared Vision	Inherited values passed down from previous generations	Participatory neighborhood associations, interfaith organizations	Regional workforce development strategies	Building economic capacity
Collaboration and Inclusion	Parents as Teachers, adult literacy programs, school activity nights for families	After-school tutoring programs, Head Start, networks of lending associations, police–community partnerships, Habitat for Humanity, soup kitchens, Salvation Army, Red Cross	Regional workforce development, incubators for small businesses, school-to-work programs, training programs, multisector partnerships, cooperatives	Economic empowerment zones

Social Systems

BUILDING COMMUNITIES OF PRACTICE

The challenge for teachers is finding ways to build community among their students' families. One idea borrowed from the work of Fetterman (2002) is to develop empowerment practices to create communities where there is little or no violence. The first step is to establish a shared vision of what the neighborhood and its institutions, namely the schools, would be like if they were violence-free. Community members then take stock of community assets, as described in this chapter, as they are brought to bear on the issue of violence. Through these two sets of data, the community finds where there are missing processes, elements, and programs, and where already existing social capital can be brought to bear on these missing pieces. Finally, empowerment practice should focus on the investment of early childhood and family development programs that can promote healthy families and develop appropriate family skills, at all levels of the social context, from immediate family structures to the larger societal culture. Communities should invest in programs that are school based or school linked so that families will become an integral part of the educational process of their children and the community, resulting in reinvestment by families in the workforce of the community. Parent involvement at all levels of the social context is imperative if social capital is to be built and to remain in the community. Thus, empowerment practice can create communities of practice where people interact more intensively with others in the community, hold their actions accountable (Fetterman, 2002), create self-evaluation, and draw on the social capital in the community.

REFERENCES

Bronfenbrenner, U. (1979). *The ecology of human development*. Boston: Harvard University Press.

Chaskin, R. J. (2001). Building community capacity. *Urban Affairs Review, 36*(3), 291–324.

Coleman, J. S. (1988). Social capital in the creation of human capital. *American Journal of Sociology, 94*, 95–120.

Crenshaw, E., & St. John, C. (1989). The organizationally dependent community: A comparative study of neighborhood attachment. *Urban Affairs Quarterly, 24*(3), 412–433.

Fetterman, D. M. (2002). Empowerment evaluation: Building communities of practice and a culture of learning. *American Journal of Community Psychology, 30*(1), 89–98.

Garbarino, J. (1995). *Raising children in a socially toxic environment.* San Francisco: Jossey-Bass.

Glickman, N., & Servon, L. (1997). *More than bricks and sticks: What is community development capacity?* New Brunswick, NJ: Center for Urban Policy Research.

Guest, A. M., & Lee, B. A. (1983). The social organization of local areas. *Urban Research Quarterly, 19*(2), 217–240.

Mattessich, P., & Monsey, B. (1997). *Community building: What makes it work, a review of factors influencing successful community building.* St. Paul, MN: Amherst H. Wilder Foundation.

McMillian, D. W., & Chavis, D. M. (1986). Sense of community: A definition and theory. *Journal of Community Psychology, 14,* 6–23.

Potapchuk, W. R., Crocker, J. P., & Schecter, W. H. (1997). Building community with social capital: Chits and chimes or chats with change. *National Civic Review, 86*(2), 129–140.

Putnam, R. D. (1993). The prosperous community: Social capital and public life. *American Prospect, 13,* 35–42.

Suttles, G. D. (1972). *The social construction of communities.* Chicago: University of Chicago Press.

Part II

USING CLASSROOM RESEARCH TO FOSTER POSITIVE VALUES

CHAPTER 5

What Is Action Research?

Action research is a systematic and valid methodology for bringing about curricular changes at a localized, decentralized, and individualized level (Jain & Benton, 1999). Each teacher is able to select the issues and problems pertinent to his or her classroom and work toward their resolution in an organized and systematic fashion. Action research helps teachers learn how to value their own work and how to give a scientific framework to their hypotheses, both their testing and implications. A brief overview of the steps in the action research process follows:

Step 1: Identify the concern.
Step 2: Collect information about the concern by generating possible reasons for the existence of the concern, developing a hypothesis based on one of the reasons, conducting a variety of benchmarks to determine where to start the intervention, and finding research related to the problem.
Step 3: Design an intervention.
Step 4: Implement the intervention.
Step 5: Collect data from the results of the intervention, using triangulation.
Step 6: Evaluate and assess the effectiveness of the intervention based on comparison of pre- and postintervention benchmark data.
Step 7: Reflect on the implications of the intervention.
Step 8: Reflect on the overall process.
Step 9: Begin the cycle again by identifying a new or continuing area of concern.

This process becomes continuous, with one action research concluding and the implications indicating needs in other areas, more interventions, and more action research.

STEP 1: IDENTIFY THE CONCERN

The action research process starts with teachers reflecting on the situation in their classrooms and the subsequent writing of a thoughtful narrative about a pressing professional concern, in this case disruptive or violent behavior. In this way, teachers can focus on their values, motives, thoughts, ideas, and understandings of the concern as well as the reasons the issue is of concern to them in their classroom. This is best accomplished by using a reflective research journal.

The reflective research journal is an integral part of the research process. Its first job is to focus the classroom teacher on what is to be investigated. The journal can have many purposes: to develop understanding of the problem; to observe the situation so as to understand it in its complexity; and to develop one's thinking through brainstorming within the context of the classroom, the school, or the community. Reflective thought is integral to the process and should become an automatic response to each action that is taken. Critical, creative, and divergent thinking all become part of the reflective thought process.

It has been found that use of a research journal can enhance not only the action research process but the end result as well, where using authentic "voice" to create dialogue is an important aspect of classroom interaction. It is the journal that begins teachers' progress in developing powerful conversations within themselves, their colleagues, and the power structure. It is the journal that can help teachers understand the many voices they use in their educational practice.

STEP 2: COLLECT INFORMATION ABOUT THE CONCERN

With a research focus decided, then comes the need to collect information about the issue, which can be derived from several types of sources: the personal reflections and responses of the person directly involved in the research; the observations of third parties; other types of data (e.g., interviews, surveys, oral or written tests); and research articles on the topic. By bringing colleagues into the classroom to observe the situation, the teacher adds other sets of eyes and ears and other valuing perspectives. Up to this point, the teacher has been reflecting on the situation alone; by involving other colleagues, the teacher also brings in new sources of data. Interviews and surveys do not need to be limited to the classroom or school. If the area of concern is thought to spill over into the community, then parents and community leaders should also become part of the process. Through these pieces of data, the teacher can begin generating possible reasons for the existence of the concern, begin developing plausible hypotheses, and conduct further benchmarks if needed. The data give the teacher the starting point for the research intervention. Some questions the teacher can reflect on include the following:

- What do you think are the causes of this concern in your classroom?
- Why do you think it needs to be tackled by a special intervention?
- How is this going to help you become a better teacher?
- How do you think this would help your students learn better?
- Which of the causes will you explore during your intervention?
- Which cause will you use to form your hypothesis?

While it is very important that teachers start with the areas of concern to them, it is also equally important that they consult the research literature to find out what, if any, information already exists on the problem they have defined as their action research area. These articles have the potential of assisting teachers in many ways. They can indicate the problem's relative importance in schooling practices and broaden their perspectives of the problem. While not necessarily describing the same processes directly that the teacher has decided to follow, the articles could indicate transferable ideas to be utilized and generate new and improved ways of thinking about the problem and possible interventions.

The benchmark data will assist in quantifying the problem, structuring the intervention, and finding a starting place, as well as help identify inherent strengths and weaknesses in processes and content. They will also lend themselves to comparisons at the end of the intervention (i.e., essentially pre- and postintervention benchmarks). It is best if the data are turned into some form of summative chart or graph so that comparisons at the end of the intervention can be clearly made. It is recognized that teachers intuitively do action research all the time, but by writing it down, keeping track of the starting and ending points, and noting in formal fashion the exact gains made by students, it is much easier to see the progress made by students and to gauge the success of the interventions.

STEP 3: DESIGN AN INTERVENTION

Begin developing strategies and plans for the intervention by analyzing the baseline data. Summarize the results by reporting, in detail, what each benchmark reveals. Discuss the number and types of students, parents, or other people who were part of the data collected. What clues do the data yield as to how curriculum may need to be strengthened or changed? What aspects of pedagogy might need to be changed? If working on a schoolwide issue, what needs to be done?

Strategies to get at the issues should begin to emerge from baseline data and provide direction for the intervention. If working in the classroom, what types of activities and lessons do the data indicate would be useful? If working with parents and the community, what types and levels of activity might be utilized?

Develop a plan for the intervention. It is best to write a full description of what the intervention will be and the materials that will be used to carry it out. If working in the classroom, this should be a daily process. If working on a schoolwide issue, this will involve a different approach, depending on what issues are being studied.

For the action research to yield reliable and valid data, it is best to triangulate the data collection to be used during the intervention period, which ideally should run the course of at least one semester. Triangulation of data occurs when different types of data are collected from different sources. For example, observations of colleagues or other individuals, interviews, the teacher's own reflections, surveys, tests, and exams all constitute data sources. But by using colleagues' observations, one's own reflections, and some type of survey or test, you have created data from different sources, which will represent different viewpoints, valuing perspectives, and interpretations. In this way, no data are skewed in one direction nor unduly influenced by one source. If another colleague will come in and observe, develop an observation sheet or checklist that the person(s) will fill out. Think about what is critical to be observed (e.g., behaviors of the pupils, teaching style, teacher–pupil or pupil–pupil interaction, curricular processes, or curricular content).

STEP 4: IMPLEMENT THE INTERVENTION

The intervention to be implemented should complement what is already part of the curriculum and classroom routine. Class activities should be integrated into other course content as much as possible, not only to allow for the normal flow of classroom processes to continue but also to achieve an integrative process so that it becomes a normal and natural part of the everyday classroom processes. Class activities should be constant, consistent, and perpetual so that students begin to anticipate and look forward to these activities.

If observing parents and community issues, develop ways of getting triangulated data that will enhance what is happening in the classroom and school and that are, again, integrative processes. If we are to begin to bring the home–community–school paradigm closer together, this would be a perfect time to consider this type of intervention.

STEP 5: COLLECT DATA FROM THE RESULTS OF THE INTERVENTION

All data should be collated, synthesized, and analyzed at this point. Postintervention data should be compared with preintervention data to discern differences in outcomes. Some questions to consider follow:

- Did the outcomes support the hypothesis? How?
- What patterns of behavior and/or responses emerged from each data source?

- Do each of the data sources agree on the outcomes?
- What kinds of changes in knowledge, attitudes, feelings, behaviors, or skills in the teacher, parents, pupils, or community emerged?
- How can the findings from the data be summarized to be made available to the pupils, parents, colleagues, and community?

STEP 6: EVALUATE AND ASSESS THE EFFECTIVENESS OF THE INTERVENTION

The following questions can help guide the evaluation and assessment of the effectiveness of the intervention and the entire action research process. Answers to these questions can be used to guide personal reflections, to compare and contrast your action research processes and approaches with those of colleagues, and to gather new ideas about how to expand and conduct further research on the same topic or develop new areas for exploration.

- Formulation of hypothesis: How clearly identified was the area of concern?
- Research articles: How many articles were collected? How useful were they in providing direction for your research study? How will they be incorporated into future action research?
- Benchmark: What type of benchmark was used? How useful was the type of data it yielded? If it was to be revised, how would it be done and why?
- Strategy/plan: How specifically designed and well planned was the intervention strategy? How well did the schedule and sequence of activities flow? Next time, what could be done differently in designing and planning the action research?
- Intervention process: What type of intervention was used? How useful was it in producing the desired changes? If it was to be revised, how would it be done and why?
- Observation checklist: What type of checklist was used? How useful was the type of data it yielded? If it was to be revised, how would it be done and why?

- Materials: What types of materials were used during the intervention? How useful were they in producing the desired results and purposes of the intervention? If they were to be revised, how would it be done and why?
- Utilization of theoretical approaches: What theoretical approaches were utilized in the action research? To what degree did they improve pedagogy? In developing future action research, how could even more effective use be made of these theoretical aspects?
- Utilization of democratic classroom processes: What democratic classroom processes were used? In what ways did they empower the pupils? In what ways did they help reduce disruptive and violent behavior? In future studies, how could even more effective use be made of them?
- Utilization of peer/pair learning: What types of peer/pair learning were used? In what ways did the intervention inculcate cooperative learning and positive interdependence? In future studies, how could these processes be utilized even more effectively? In what ways did they help reduce disruptive and violent behavior?
- Prejudice reduction: What types of activities were used to reduce prejudice? In what ways did the intervention actually reduce pupils' intercultural prejudices? In the future, what further activity could be used to create even more effectiveness? In what ways did they help reduce disruptive and violent behavior?
- Relevance of intervention: In what ways was the intervention developmentally appropriate and curriculum specific? How could changes be made to enhance its relevance?
- Meaningful research: In what ways has this action research validated your teaching and empowered you and your colleagues?
- Collegial inquiry: In what ways has this action research promoted collegial inquiry, support, and space for instructional innovation?
- Reflective practice: How well did you reflect and analyze the results of your research study to (1) understand its implications (positive or negative), (2) help you identify future direction from which to launch your next level of action research, and (3) assist you in giving meaning, direction, and redefinition to your teaching practice?

STEP 7: REFLECT ON THE IMPLICATIONS OF THE INTERVENTION

Many focal points can be used to reflect on the success of the intervention. One can focus on the empowerment of the students or perhaps how they were delimited by the intervention. Another focus could be how meaningful the research was to the teacher and whether or not it validated the teacher's practice. Reflection could also focus on how the intervention promoted collegial inquiry or to what degree preservice teachers benefited from it. The following questions can guide this phase of the action research process:

- How and to what degree did the intervention empower students, through one or more of the following: (1) democratic classrooms (participatory governance, student choice, positive feedback, ownership), (2) critical thinking (analytical, reflective), (3) cooperative learning (peer learning, pair learning, teamwork, leadership, positive interdependence), (4) prejudice reduction, and (5) the reduction of disruptive and violent behavior?
- How has this action research accelerated learning achievement in your classroom? To what extent and percentage?
- How and to what degree did the intervention delimit students?
- How did the intervention produce meaningful research? To what extent was it relevant and useful to your needs in the classroom?
- How did the intervention build self-esteem and confidence and validate the teacher's practice?
- How did the intervention promote collegial inquiry and teacher leadership?
- How did the intervention promote academic innovation and support within the system?

STEP 8: REFLECT ON THE OVERALL PROCESS

As teachers are increasingly asked to produce results according to outcomes-based processes, action research and reflective thinking, in supporting systematic examination of classroom practice, take on more important roles in the process of education. Therefore, it is also important for teachers to reflect on the overall process of action research. The following questions can assist in this reflection:

- How did the action research help in widening your horizons, your critical thinking, and your problem-solving processes?
- What impact did this study have on the way you will teach in the future: the way you will create success and high achievement in your students, the way you will change your curriculum, the way you will continue to reduce disruptive behavior and violence?
- What implications does this action research have for other educators and the way they construct their curriculum?
- If you found that other teachers became interested in your research, describe this interaction. What implications does this have for collegial inquiry and teacher empowerment?
- Do you think this process of action research has brought about an attitudinal change in yourself, other teachers, and school officials?

STEP 9: BEGIN THE CYCLE AGAIN BY IDENTIFYING A NEW OR CONTINUING AREA OF CONCERN

Key to the process of using action research is the continuity of the cycle. It is this action—plan, act, reflect—that is integral to best practices since there is a constant renewal of the process. The results of one action research should lead to the next, a process that should become thoroughly integrated into each teacher's modus operandi. This is absolutely necessary given the fact that teachers now need to produce visible results in the classroom. Some questions to guide the teacher into the next cycle of the action research process are listed as follows:

- What kinds of problems did you run into while implementing your action research, and how did you cope with them?
- What kinds of problems did you experience in collecting several kinds of data, and how did you cope with this?
- What new questions were raised as a result of doing this action research?
- What new issues have emerged?

- What new action research could be mounted as a result of these new questions that have emerged?

In summary, action research produces visible results that can be documented for accrediting agencies and for use within the community. It offers teachers opportunities for constant renewal through perpetual examination of and reflection on their teaching practice. Further, by validating their practice, teachers can provide the leadership in schools and communities to seek workable and effective solutions to issues of pressing concern such as those addressed in this book.

REFERENCE

Jain, N., & Benton, J. (1999). A comparative study of teaching practices in the United States and India which promote intercultural understanding and awareness. In K. Häkkinen (Ed.), *Innovative approaches to intercultural education* (pp. 75–108). Jyväskylä, Finland: University of Jyväskylä Press.

CHAPTER 6

Formulating Plans to Develop Peaceful Classrooms

In the formulation of curricula and activities that foster positive social values and limit disruptive behavior, sense needs to be made of the numerous interventions that have been developed to promote nonviolence. Galtung's (1976) taxonomy of processes for promoting peace is useful for developing awareness of what interventions are available and how they work. In this taxonomy, he identifies three levels of action used to resolve conflict: *peacekeeping*, *peacemaking*, and *peace building*. Integrated into these various categories are violence reduction initiatives at the federal, state, and local levels. These include legislation of state laws, such as the 1994 Gun-Free Schools Act, to hold parents legally responsible for their children's behavior. Local community initiatives include a range of family services provided by religious and recreational organizations, social services, and public housing and health agencies. The most effective programs are those that involve the community and the schools working together (Schwartz, 1996).

In classrooms and schools, *peacekeeping* would be defined as the use of force to keep control of the environment. Strategies such as metal detectors, police presence, ID badges, "zero tolerance" policies, threat of punishment and punitive action, weapons searches, in-school suspension (ISS), drug awareness programs (e.g., DARE), expelling students who bring weapons to school, trying youth offenders as adults, reducing the availability of guns, and removing victims from the situations are all peacekeeping methods making parents legally responsible for truancy and delinquency of their children. While some of these interventions might be useful initially to restore order, the end result of these types of initiatives is to turn off students to school and to perpetuate violence in response to problems. The main reason these initiatives' have limited success and sustainability is that students, faculty, and parents are not given any skills to solve problems.

Peacemaking uses communication to resolve conflicts. Strategies in this category include peer mediation and conflict resolution, Behavior Intervention Support Team (BIST), accountability for teacher-made rules, and teacher-led conflict resolution. This method of violence reduction is widely used and has shown success in certain situations. Peacemaking has at its core communication, which teaches young people and others how to resolve conflicts and mediate disputes through use of dialogue, as opposed to actions directed toward one another. Conflict resolution, though, is not culturally neutral (Myers & Filner, 1994) but instead is designed for cultures accustomed to openly confronting issues (i.e., Western cultures), which is not common behavior in collectivist cultures (Ting-Toomey, 1985). The question, then, is who benefits? If those who are typically dominated participate in the conflict resolution process, then they may accept a resolution that does not serve their needs, which could cause continued resentment, feelings of hostility, and continued violence. Also, agreements that avoid conflicts fail to create a sustainable peace because they do not overcome the problem (Carter, 2002). Rather, the problem becomes suppressed, only to bubble up again at any time. Where peacemaking falls short is that it is essentially a behavioral process that, while potentially beneficial, does not change fundamental valuing structures. The focus of peacemaking is to medicate the symptoms, not address the root causes of the disease.

Peacemaking brings us a step closer to providing sustained violence reduction, but it does not yet create an intrinsic valuing of peace and nonviolent behavior, nor develop a proactive stance toward peace. Where this set of strategies works best is in an environment where common values and belief systems are at work (i.e., in monocultural environments). With the increasing diversity of this country, it is virtually impossible to find such environments. Therefore, extreme care must be taken to ensure that all students' cultural values and processes of interaction and communication are fully represented in conflict resolution disputes. Also, representation on conflict resolution panels by students of various cultures is a necessity if all students are to receive fair and equitable treatment. With the equitable representation of all students culturally (gender, ethnicity, race, socioeconomic levels, linguistic differences, and so on), building successful communication between and among different cultural groups becomes possible.

Peace building has the potential to empower its participants and create avenues for violence reduction. Strategies in this category include teaching social competence, developing understanding and recognition of emotions in selves and others, helping children respond appropriately to critical incidents, learning how to predict consequences of acts, selecting and nurturing positive peer relationships, providing for caring and democratic classrooms, modeling of peaceful behaviors by teachers and students acting as partners in and sharing responsibility for the teaching–learning process, peer teaching, peer tutoring, book buddies, student literacy coaches, positive interdependence, cooperative learning, active listening, class meetings, self-esteem building, collaborative processes for rule making, teaching the principles of problem solving, active cooperation between parents and schools and larger interagency responses, and opportunities for children to participate in service learning.

Peace building is a proactive strategy that builds a "peace consciousness" and creates the conditions for sustained nonviolence and lasting conflict resolution. Harris (1996) identified key areas of educational practice to implement peace-building strategies on a schoolwide level.

- Content: Students study nonviolence, peace, ecological sustainability, and struggles for justice. They tell stories of peace heroes and heroines and engage in peace projects and activities. They study conflicts that range from simple disagreements to wars. They learn to identify problems and seek alternative solutions to problems. They learn about the interconnectedness of all life.
- Feelings: Students take part in support groups; learn how to be peer counselors; and utilize feelings of compassion, calmness, and confidence to build skills of charity, forgiveness, empathy, and community building. Students are provided a safe environment to ventilate their concerns about violence. Feelings are put to use to create peace-building skills.

- Skills: Students are taught communication skills. They learn about caring, tolerance, cooperation, impulse control, anger management, and taking perspective.
- Discipline: Teachers model how to help students respect limits, set boundaries, and take responsibility for behavior.
- Pedagogy: Teachers empower students to solve conflict nonviolently by using cooperative learning methodologies and collaborative tasks, setting up democratic classrooms, and using problem-solving techniques. It also includes teachers modeling respect for differences, showing affirmation, and creating space for dialogue.
- Motivation: Educators offset the attractiveness of violence by motivating students to value peace. They help students organize programs, assemblies, and other social activities to focus on solutions to problems and recognize peace leaders. Students share stories and create collaborative peace projects.
- Administration: Most important, leadership in promoting a commitment and vision of nonviolence must come from administration. A school run on the previously described principles is democratic and relies on site-based management, where all staff have a say in how the school is to be administered. This type of school is inclusive and builds rapport with parents and the community to address problems of violence. (Harris, 1996)

While this list is comprehensive and a good start in creating a peace education curriculum, it falls short in its conspicuous absence of concept building, a process that must come before all the other aspects. It is this beginning process that initializes shifts in the valuing system. Key concepts of peace and nonviolence such as justice and injustice must be thoroughly understood; youths must be grounded in these concepts first before internalization and intrinsic valuing of peace can occur.

How, then, should teachers go about building peace education initiatives? The only peace education curriculum that will work is one that uses the peace-building concept yet begins with concept development through content exploration and then develops complex equality through pedagogical and administrative practices (see figure 6.1). By focusing on these four spheres, positive feelings (dispositions) toward peace will naturally develop, motivation will be high, and discipline will be a moot point.

Concept: Concept building is the first phase. A knowledge base about the concept and its components—principles, subconcepts, theories, and definitions—needs to be gained through use of examples understandable to students at their developmental levels and within their realms of experience. For example, using the concept of justice, the following must be taught and understood: theories of justice, definitions of justice and injustice, justified exclusion, internal exclusion, insider versus outsider, the principle of utility, agencies of inclusion, and complex equality. Other concepts that could be explored include social justice, representation, and self-determination.

Concept-embedded content: Students must build a knowledge base of critical incidents, both from historical sources and current events, in which the concept is prevalent in order to explore aspects of the concept, and its negative side as well. For example, incidents from the Civil Rights Era or from Gandhi's life will bring to light all of the previously mentioned concepts. By putting the concepts into context through critical incidents, students will learn to recognize instances of justice and injustice.

CONCEPT
⇩
CONCEPT-EMBEDDED CONTENT
⇩
USE OF CONCEPT
⇩
SKILLS ⇨ **APPLICATION OF CONCEPT** ⇦ PEDAGOGICAL PRACTICES
⇧
ADMINISTRATIVE PRACTICES

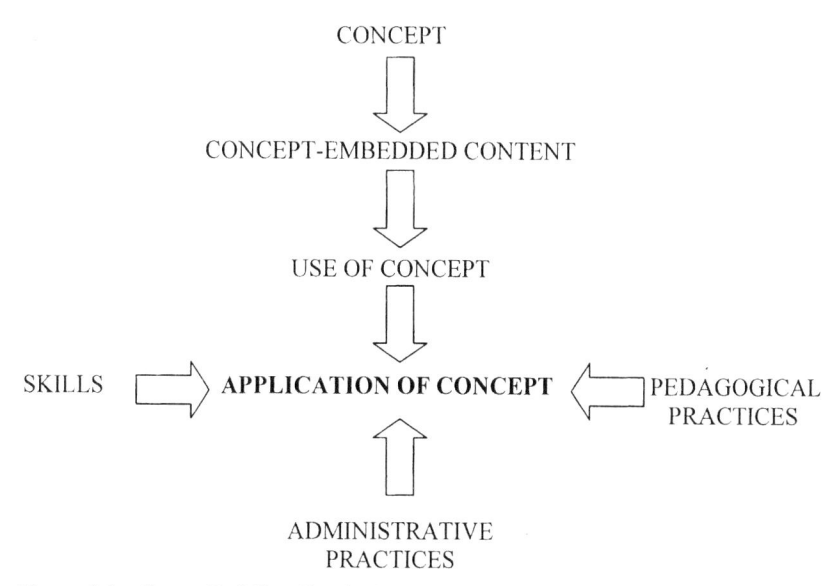

Figure 6.1. Peace-Building Curriculum Framework

Use of concept: Students are now guided in the use of the concept by searching for critical incidents happening in their community, their state, their country, or abroad. Through guidance from the teacher, they learn how to use the concept correctly in all of its contexts.

Application of concept: Students at this level are now ready to develop their own school-based problem to work on in the realm of nonviolence and peace. They understand the concept and its components and are able to apply them to their own scenario.

Skills: As students begin to develop their own school-based problem, the teacher should gradually begin introducing peace-based skills to the students, such as active listening, cooperation, tolerance, caring, empathy, compassion, perspective taking, imagination, and creativity.

Pedagogical practices: Practices the teacher should use to structure the students' work on their school-based problem should include democratic classroom practices such as cooperative learning, peer and paired learning, positive interdependence, participatory governance, student choice, positive feedback, and ownership. Other equally important practices are reflective thinking, critical thinking, problem solving, and using multiple intelligences.

Administrative practices: These practices should include democratic site-based management, shared governance, and support for the development and activation of a peace education curriculum.

By using the four spheres of practice and aspects of peace outlined by Groff (2002)—the absence of war, the balance of forces in the international system, the elimination of direct and structural violence at various levels (individual, group, and nation), intercultural peace, and Gaia peace, which regards the earth as a sacred, living being—a holistic set of school-based peace and nonviolence principles can be derived and developed, as follows:

- Nonviolent behavior
- Shared governance of the school (students, teachers, administration, and community)
- Equal access to resources and respect for all
- Complex equality—the idea that everyone has something to offer, share, and give to the school community and, therefore, should be celebrated

- Respectful and responsible stewardship of the school buildings, grounds, classrooms, and community

It is through these practices and initiatives, then, that a *peace-building curriculum* can be produced for the twenty-first century in order to transform the present culture of violence into a culture of peace for our children and their children.

In the following chapters, successful case studies in peacemaking and peace building are presented in detail, in a way that teachers can replicate these interventions in their classrooms.

Following are resources for implementing peace-building curriculum:

Stories of Peace. Ann Mason, Pulteney Grammar School, Adelaide, Australia (Pulteney.sa.edu.au). Peace education is about everybody working with peaceful processes at each and every level of daily living. The classroom is the perfect place to begin the peace process. Time should be set aside for open debate and discussion, for the establishment of processes for compromise and negotiation, and for learning and practicing appropriate techniques. Questioning and researching what peace and happiness mean to people of other countries and cultures can invite deep or sensitive commentary from children. Constructing web pages and presenting students' peace writings on class web pages is a good way to share successes in promoting peace throughout the world via cyberspace.

Imagine Peace. Hassaun Jones-Bey encourages us to share stories of peace (www.imaginepeace.org).

Practices That Make School a Place of Peace. National Council for Teacher Education, India (www.ncte-in.org/pub/unesco/ch5.htm). Useful peace education practices discussed on this site include developing codes of conduct for classes and schools; developing a school discipline guide; strategies for developing self-esteem; using special activities and exercises for developing peaceful competencies; moral instruction to start the day; school and classroom wallpaper to portray essays, short stories, and articles with peace as a central concept; displaying peace mottos; appointing class mediators and a peace committee; a peace-inspired morning assembly; and school link programs.

Canadian School Weaves Web of Peace (www.education-world.com), prekindergarten to sixth grade. Student artwork and poetry focus on six principles of a culture of peace and nonviolence: respect all life, reject violence, share with others, listen to understand, preserve the planet, and rediscover solidarity.

Peace Pole Project Peace Pals (e-pals) (www.worldpeace.org) "May peace prevail on Earth" written in various languages on peace poles planted throughout the world. Provides a daily reminder of keeping peaceful lives in classrooms and at home. Peace Pals fosters understanding and respect for diversity through a variety of activities.

Eleven Principles of Effective Character Education (www.character.org/principles). Two principles especially help develop nonviolence. Principle 2: Character must be comprehensively defined to include thinking, feeling, and behavior. Good character involves understanding, caring about, and acting appropriately when encountering ethical values. Students should grow as they learn more about their community and how to act upon it. Principle 5: To develop character, students need opportunity for moral action. Students are constructive learners; they learn best by being provided opportunities to apply values (e.g., how to divide the labor in a group activity, how to reach consensus during a classroom discussion, how to carry out a community service project, how to reduce fights on a playground).

Circles of Peace (www.salsa.net/peace). Website inviting students, teachers, and activists to break cycles of violence through circles of peace.

Peace Games (www.peacegames.org/). Provides children and families with skills, language, and supportive relationships to create safe schools and combat violence and racism.

REFERENCES

Carter, C. (2002). Conflict resolution at school: Building compassionate communities. *Social Alternatives, 21*(1), 49–55.

Galtung, J. (1976). Peacekeeping, peacemaking, and peace building. In J. Galtung (Ed.), *Peace, war, and defense* (pp. 282–305). Copenhagen: Christian Ejlers.

Groff, L. (2002). A holistic view of peace education. *Social Alternatives, 21*(1), 7–10.

Harris, I. M. (1996). From world peace to peace in the 'hood. *Journal for a Just and Caring Education, 2*(4), 378–396.

Myers, S., & Filner, B. (1994). *Mediation across cultures: A handbook about conflict and culture.* Amherst, MA: Amherst Educational.

Schwartz, W. (1996). An overview of strategies to reduce school violence. *ERIC/CUE Digest, 115,* 1–7.

Ting-Toomey, S. (1985). Toward a theory of conflict and culture. In W. B. Gudykunst, L. P. Stewart, and S. Ting-Toomey (Eds.), *Communication, culture and organizational processes: International and intercultural communication annual, vol. 4* (pp. 71–86). Thousand Oaks, CA: Sage.

Part III

CASE STUDIES IN BEST PRACTICES

CHAPTER 7

Conflict Resolution and Peer Mediation

As disruptive, aggressive, and often violent behavior appears with increasing frequency in school settings, effective schoolwide responses are critical to ensure both student and teacher safety and to produce young people who are able to cope effectively in a complex and fast-paced world. Punitive reactions to these inappropriate behaviors are only temporary fixes because they do not teach these young people how to cope in the long term. Thus, conflict resolution and peer mediation programs in school settings can lead the way to helping this segment of young people lead productive and fulfilling lives. These programs have been found to provide students with a framework for resolving conflicts (Deutsch, 1994), give students an opportunity to assume responsibility for their own behavior (Schrumpf, Crawford, & Usadel, 1991), lower teacher stress by reducing the number of student conflicts they have to handle (Benson & Benson, 1993), increase instructional time (Benson & Benson, 1993), and help students understand how cultural diversity can affect interpersonal communication and human interactions (Girard & Koch, 1996).

Daunic, Smith, Robinson, Landry, and Miller (1999) found that conflict resolution and peer mediation programs in tandem can result in positive, lasting changes in school climate, especially when schools have administrators and teachers committed to the process. The central premise of their research was that conflict is an inevitable part of any social environment and that students can successfully address conflict through a problem-solving framework. Their curriculum was designed to teach students to acknowledge individual difference, change win–lose paradigms to win–win solutions, and use negotiation to resolve conflicts. The peer mediation portion of their program was a structured process consisting of specific steps to help students in conflict with one another to define and solve a problem.

Table 7.1 outlines the keys to a successful peer mediation program.

CONFLICT RESOLUTION CASE STUDY

The following case study describes one second grade teacher's (Mrs. K's) successful attempt at resolving conflict in her classroom. Through the process of action research, she was able to perceive the problem in a different light and successfully find a way to create peace in her classroom (see table 7.2). Her approach followed the steps identified in chapter 5 on action research processes.

Step 1: Identify the Concern

During observations of the students in her classroom, Mrs. K noticed that the girls had a great deal more difficulty getting along and working together than the boys did. In this classroom of fifteen students, the five girls always seemed to have something stirring. It was often about

Table 7.1. Keys to a Successful Peer Mediation Program

Start early	It is important for young children to learn "that's how we do it at school." By the time they are ready for middle school, they will know how to refer themselves to mediation to settle disputes instead of resorting to name-calling and fighting.
Teach problem-solving skills to all students	Commit to finding and using a curriculum that helps students see advantages to problem solving and gives them simple tools to accomplish this on their own or with the help of others.
Make mediation part of a comprehensive program	Work together as a staff to create violence-prevention programs that include student-initiated problem solving.
Model mediation skills	Have all staff learn, teach, and model the skills required of student mediators.
Involve community	Invite community volunteers to train along with students and serve as adult coaches for student mediators.

Source: Angaran & Beckwith (1999).

Table 7.2. Using Action Research to Resolve Conflict

Problem	Research	Hypothesis/Baseline	Intervention
Conflicts between girls getting more frequent and more emotional	Angaran & Beckwith, 1999; Benson & Benson, 1993; Bodine, Crawford, & Schrumpf, 1994; Daunic, Smith, Robinson, & Miller, 2000; Deutsch, 1994; Girard & Koch, 1996; Schrumpf, Crawford, & Usudel, 1991	If students are taught to use reflective thinking techniques, conflicts will occur less frequently during school activities.	Daily lessons teaching children how to deal with conflict, involving children's literature, role-playing, art, puzzles, songs, poetry, and discussion groups

Observations	Postintervention Findings	Implications	Reflections
Colleagues Preservice practicum students College supervisor	Postintervention data found a significantly lower number of conflicts during the intervention period. Data collected did not support initial hypothesis that girls were having more difficulty getting along than boys.	Students learned how to use reflective thought processes to handle conflict and gained greater identity of themselves and how they fit into the larger society.	Action research is a process that can help teachers, staff, and students gain answers to unknown questions and is a wonderful tool to validate pedagogical techniques implemented in class. The undergraduates' assistance helped reduce the teacher's workload on research time. Implementing the process encourages collegiality and teacher–student empowerment.

Direction for New Cycle of Action Research

The time frame for the project needs to be extended. The project needs to be replicated in other classrooms, schools, and communities.

something very trivial, but many times this led to a conflict that ended up with one or several of them crying or saying mean things to one another. Sometimes these little quarrels lasted for a few minutes, sometimes for days. Mrs. K tried breaking up these little spats, but it only seemed to provide temporary results. The conflicts in this group of five girls began very early in the year, and by midyear, the teacher found these disagreements getting more frequent and emotional, and the girls were now teaming up against one another. Rarely a day went by that one of the girls did not create a scene by pouting or crying. In addition to the problems becoming more frequent, these episodes extended onto the playground and to special-subject classrooms such as art and music. Mrs. K noticed the girls using words and actions with each other that were not healthy and that hurt each other's feelings and lowered self-esteem.

Step 2: Collect Information about the Concern

For the benchmark data, the teacher kept a checklist of observations on the students in her second grade classroom for at least one week prior to the intervention strategies. Mrs. K noted the students' names, behaviors and conflicts exhibited, and where these behaviors took place. She then reviewed this checklist to see if she could find a pattern to when these conflicts were occurring. She recorded forty-three incidents of undesirable student behavior during this week. The teacher reasoned that if her students were taught to use reflective thinking techniques, conflicts would occur less frequently.

The research articles collected by the teacher and her undergraduate team reflected a diverse array of perspectives on conflict resolution. Among the various ideas gathered from the research that the team felt were important were the following key points:

- Conflict resolution is an effective tool for the types of problems arising in schools today.
- There are step-by-step principles to be followed: separate the students from the problem, focus on interests, invent options for mutual gain, and use objective criteria.
- Use of peer mediators and neutral third parties can be beneficial in the intervention process.

- Telling a story from another person's viewpoint (e.g., through using fairy tales) can also produce positive results.
- Examining other people's viewpoints and trying to reach agreement on those points of view can create effective solutions.
- Reflective thinking can be an important tool in resolving conflicts.
- Cooperative problem solving and positive communication promote reflective thinking and peer mediation automatically when taught and enforced at a young age.

Step 3: Design an Intervention

By reviewing the literature about using conflict resolution in the classroom, Mrs. K discovered many ways to help children learn how to deal with differences. Of four approaches detailed by Bodine, Crawford, and Schrumpf (1994), she decided to rework and adapt their process curriculum to fit her own situation. The process curriculum approach is characterized by devoting time to teaching children how to use problem-solving methods and then teaching them how to reflect on these decisions and outcomes.

Mrs. K selected mini-lessons that involved the use of children's literature and role-playing activities that would encourage children to explore their feelings and abilities to resolve problems by themselves. She also decided to focus on teachable moments throughout the day. If the topic of the mini-lesson was being happy, then she would stress and talk about "happy" activities throughout the day. She would then ask the children to discuss their feelings about these activities.

Since Mrs. K had many years of experience with children of this age group, she was well aware that the intervention would be more effective if she involved the students in hands-on activities where they could freely express themselves. Therefore, she assumed the role of a coach by encouraging children in their interactions with other students to use care in their choice of words and actions.

Step 4: Implement the Intervention

During the first two weeks of the intervention, Mrs. K centered her activities around ideas to help students deal with different kinds of emotions (e.g., happiness, sadness, fear, loneliness, and shame). She had the students use puzzles, children's literature, songs, poetry, discussion groups, and role-playing to explore a variety of feelings that people go through. Then she related these feelings to everyday happenings. She encouraged the students to talk about whatever they had on their minds.

During the next two weeks, Mrs. K focused on helping the students understand the importance of getting along and solving conflicts. Using Bodine, Crawford, and Schrumpf's (1994) six-step process for solving conflicts (setting the stage, gathering perspectives, identifying needs, creating options, evaluating the options, and generating agreement), she integrated these steps into her daily lessons and gradually was able to show the students how to identify their own needs and interests. She then worked with them to find solutions to each issue.

Following this, Mrs. K took up the topic of developing positive friendships by discussing characteristics of good friends and why it is important to have good friends. She also focused the discussions and activities on the importance of learning how to think through a problem and how to resolve a dispute peacefully.

Throughout the intervention period, she and her undergraduate team continued to keep the checklists. However, Mrs. K noticed that it was rather difficult for the undergraduates, who did not know the students by name, to keep track of each student and his or her behaviors. So, after a team meeting, it was decided to record the undergraduate observations in paragraph form by focusing on the conflict, noting where it took place, and giving a brief description of the children involved. Afterward, Mrs. K identified the children and filled in this information.

Other colleagues in the classroom were able to either confirm or refute the teacher's initial observations and reflections on the situation. Also, at the end of each intervention, the teacher received feedback from her students, either through pencil and paper tasks or through oral discussions. In addition, Mrs. K asked the students to keep behavior journals. In this way, the teacher had at least five reference points to constantly keep her on course and moving forward. These different sources of data prevented the intervention from reaching invalid and unreliable conclusions.

Step 5: Collect Data from the Results of the Intervention

Mrs. K used five sources of data: her own observations, observations from the undergraduate team, student behavior journals, student feedback from the activities, and pencil and paper tasks.

The combined data from both the teacher and the team observations showed a preintervention total of forty-three unacceptable behaviors and a postintervention total of seven. The data also showed that the total number of conflicts during the intervention period was twenty-nine for girls and seventy-one for boys. The number of students writing in the behavioral journals began at three, increased to five during the second week, and ended at one. The total number of girls writing in behavioral journals was two, while for boys it was nine.

The products from the specific mini-lessons and activities yielded much data, such as making a "friends web"; composing a "kindness pledge" to be recited each day; drawing self-portraits; listing things that are fun to do together; drawing "kiss pictures"; listing things that bugged them; responding to a children's literature video; role-playing bad situations such as "selfish," "teasing," and "lying" incidents and figuring out good solutions; giving warm fuzzies to other students and family members; listing talents and strengths; listing positive characteristics about friendship; and writing kind messages to a secret friend.

Step 6: Evaluate and Assess the Effectiveness of the Intervention

Mrs. K began her collection of data a week before the intervention to note the students involved in undesirable behavior, the type of behavior or conflict, and where and when the events took place. She recorded a total of forty-three incidents during the gathering of this baseline data. After reviewing this data, she found that most of the conflicts occurred during less-structured times, such as recess, learning centers, and accelerated reading time. She also noticed that most of the behaviors recorded were incidents with the boys rather than the girls. This was her first surprise!

When the postintervention data were compared with the preintervention data, Mrs. K found a significantly lower number of incidents recorded during the intervention by both her and the team. She attributed this to the following factors.

During the intervention period, Mrs. K required the students to write in behavior journals if they were involved in a severe conflict (i.e., an incident that could cause harm to themselves, another person, or to property). She reasoned that this would encourage students to take responsibility for their actions since students would have to think about the incident and translate these thoughts to paper, thus giving them time to process and realize how serious their actions were. Additionally, students also had to develop and write down a satisfactory resolution to the conflict.

Mrs. K noted that about one week into the intervention, students were able to identify behaviors and conflicts that would carry a consequence of writing in their journals. She also noted that she would often hear the students reminding each other about actions that were very dangerous.

Step 7: Reflect on the Implications of Intervention

Mrs. K's reflections revealed many things. She found the intervention to be very beneficial to both herself and the students. She felt very positive about the interventions she incorporated into her classroom and found that the students enjoyed the activities they did together, especially the role-playing.

She was very impressed with the way her students learned to work together to accomplish tasks and how very involved they were with different activities that encouraged them to think about how to handle difficult situations. She found the students eager to participate and to offer a variety of answers when investigating problem situations for possible solutions and consequences.

She was also very excited about how the students began to help and encourage each other toward the end of the intervention. Quite often she would hear the word *think* being spoken by the students; this word was used throughout the mini-lessons, activities, and at various times during the day.

Mrs. K also found that the series of mini-lessons gave her the chance to encourage the students to develop their own identities and discover how they fit into the larger society. She discussed with them how people in their classes, the school, the community, and the larger society are both alike and different and how in order to be good citizens, they need to develop an understanding of the diverse world out there waiting for them to add their wonderful contributions. She now saw the students being more aware of how their actions and reactions affected others around them; they seemed to demonstrate a greater sense of compassion and respect for one another.

As a result of this intervention, Mrs. K realized that all things were not necessarily as they appeared. While she subconsciously recognized this, the action research brought it to reality. In her initial observations she expected the girls to have more conflicts than the boys, but when she actually kept records and analyzed the data, the results were astonishing to her. In reflecting on this outcome, she decided she had made the assumption that girls were more often emotional and traumatic in their dealings with conflict, whereas boys did not tend to be as verbal, preferring instead to handle situations on their own.

Step 8: Reflect on the Overall Process

Mrs. K found the action research process very insightful. She realized that she and probably other teachers use this process on a daily basis, but not to the degree and length that she did in researching, thinking through the intervention, and documenting the data. She found that it is necessary to gather research and data to support what she and other teachers are doing in their classrooms and that through action research teachers can gain insight into what changes they need to make to create a more productive and enjoyable learning environment.

The assistance of the undergraduate team was of immense help to Mrs. K. Since research can be a lengthy and time-consuming process, and with the demands made on a classroom teacher, the teacher appreciated the undergraduates' role in identifying classroom behaviors and locating and gathering relevant research on the problem she had identified. This gave her more time to focus on the actual intervention and to observe the changes that took place in her and her students.

While working on the action research project, she also found that it brought her closer to her colleagues; who were not only curious about what she was attempting to do in her classroom but also supportive of her project by constantly bringing in ideas and providing her with encouragement. In addition, her efforts were noticed by the principal, who had observed that her students were being kinder to one another and that there was now an air of excitement in her classroom. The principal encouraged Mrs. K to continue working on her classroom issues through this action research process and encouraged her colleagues to do likewise.

Step 9: Begin the Cycle Again by Identifying a New or Continuing Area of Concern

Reflecting on the entire process and the interactions Mrs. K had experienced with students, colleagues, and undergraduate students, she concluded that she would not only attempt this again in her own classroom—with the knowledge to enhance the experience—but also encourage her colleagues and the principal to look into similar types of action research projects in their own building.

In summary, the outcome of this conflict resolution and peer mediation action research project was that the percentage of "repeat offenders" was halved, but the teacher also discovered that 80 percent of the "offences" were actually made by the boys, not the girls, as she had originally thought. In reflecting on the outcomes, Mrs. K found that her time was not wasted. The pupils not only responded positively to the activities, but they also began to help and encourage one another, to develop their own identities, and to understand how their actions and reactions affected others around them. This resulted in a growing sense of compassion and respect for one another. In trying to understand why she had overlooked the boys' conflicts, she developed more hypotheses for future interventions. Mrs. K realized that many of her assumptions about the processes of socialization needed more reflection, revision, and action. Her assumptions about girls being more traumatic and emotional in their dealings with conflicts and therefore more visible in the classroom led her to assume that the girls were the ones that needed to be straightened out. The boys often preferred less verbal and more active solutions to their problems, which meant she had not noticed them having more conflicts than the girls. Finally, she realized that the way boys and girls were socialized was not necessarily a given. All pupils needed to understand how their actions, verbal or nonverbal, reflected not only on themselves but also on the society.

In looking at other successful conflict resolution and peer mediation programs, such as those documented at the beginning of this chapter, parents and adults in the community were also involved. To extend this action research into the community would be an excellent way to involve parents and community leaders in the process of understanding how to resolve issues of disruptive, aggressive, and violent behavior in their schools and communities.

REFERENCES

Angaran, S., & Beckwith, K. (1999). Elementary school peer mediation. *Education Digest, 65,* 23–26.

Benson, A. J., & Benson, J. M. (1993). Peer mediation: Conflict resolution in schools. *Journal of School Psychology, 31,* 427–430.

Bodine, R., Crawford, D., & Schrumpf, F. (1994). *Creating the peaceable school: A comprehensive program for teaching conflict resolution.* Champaign, IL: Research Press.

Daunic, A. P., Smith, S. W., Robinson, T. R., Landry, K. L., & Miller, M. D. (2000). School-wide conflict resolution and peer mediation programs: Experience in three middle schools. *Intervention in School and Clinic, 36,* 94–100.

Deutsch, M. (1994). Constructive conflict resolution: Principles, training, and research. *Journal of Social Issues, 50,* 13–32.

Girard, K., & Koch, S. J. (1996). *Conflict resolution in the schools: A manual for educators.* San Francisco: Jossey-Bass.

Schrumpf, F., Crawford, D., & Usadel, H. C. (1991). *Peer mediation: Conflict resolution in the schools.* Champaign, IL: Research Press.

CHAPTER 8

Peer Learning, Paired Learning, and Positive Interdependence

Peer-assisted learning strategies have been utilized for more than thirty years by teachers (Viadero, 2003) to achieve a variety of positive outcomes in their students. It has been found that when children work together as partners, they spend more time exploring ideas and reorganizing information, as well as take responsibility for their learning (Walberg, 1998; Foot & Howe, 1998). They also enhance the complexity of their thinking (Vygotsky, 1978; Piaget, 1926). The largest percentage of peer and paired partnership research has focused on academic achievement as the primary goal (Richards, King, & Joseph, 2003; Fuchs, Fuchs, & Burish, 2000; Fuchs, Mathes, & Fuchs, 1995; Slavin, 1983). It has also been found that when peer tutoring is structured, gains are even greater (Cohen, Kulik, & Kulik, 1982; Kaflus, 1984; Delquadri, Greenwood, Whorton, Carta, & Hall, 1986; Franca, Kerr, Reitz, & Lambert, 1990).

Peer tutoring for social benefit is also well documented in the research. Franca et al. (1990) found that children experienced increased positive exchanges and decreased negative verbal interactions when peer tutoring situations were well structured and managed by the teacher. Johnson (1981) noted that enhanced feelings of belonging and support were facilitated by peer relationships, and cooperation and leadership skills were developed (Konner, 1976). Since joint problem solving necessitates positive behavior in the coordination and negotiation of conflict, both academic and social competencies in children are enhanced (Brownell & Carriger, 1990; Johnson, 1981; Mugny & Doise, 1978; Slavin, 1983).

86 CHAPTER 8

PEER TUTORING CASE STUDY

This case study explores the promise and practicality of using peer tutoring to improve classroom social interaction (see table 8.1). Since the students came from a variety of backgrounds and socioeconomic classes, the teacher, Mrs. A, felt that peer tutoring might create community in her classroom so that all children showed respect and concern for one another and also improve student achievement at the same time.

Step 1: Identify the Concern

In her efforts to create a more positive social environment in her kindergarten classroom and to get children to work together and learn from each other in a more constructive manner, Mrs. A had set up many activities where her children were actively engaged in their own learning. One of the tasks that students needed to complete on a daily basis was logging onto the computer. While the process was child-friendly, it was extensive and required many steps. Originally, the teacher had set a goal of having each child learn this process and complete the logging on independently. While some of the children caught on quickly, others did not. The children who encountered difficulty frequently called on the teacher to help them rather than go to their peers for help.

Mrs. A found that her children did not rely on each other for any type of assistance. If a situation arose in which a child had a question, the teacher was the first one asked for help. In the event that another child provided assistance, the child receiving the help did not respond positively to the assistance provided. She felt that the children lacked respect for one another and did not display a sense of solidarity or community when going about their tasks for the day. She was also concerned about why some of her students did not catch on quickly. Was it because they had not been exposed to technology before? Were these children in a different social class and therefore ostracized?

Step 2: Collect Information about the Concern

To gather baseline information, Mrs. A paired each child with a partner, one each with high and low ability. The children were shown the

Table 8.1. Peer and Paired Partnerships and Positive Interdependence

Problem	Research	Hypothesis/Baseline	Intervention
Children do not depend on each other for any type of assistance. The teacher is the first one a student calls on when he or she needs assistance.	Brownell & Carriger, 1990; Cohen, Kulik, & Kulik, 1982; Delquadri, Greenwood, Whorton, Carta, & Hall, 1986; Foot & Howe, 1998; Franca, Kerr, Reitz, & Lambert, 1990; Fuchs, Fuchs, & Burish, 2000; Fuchs, Mathes, &Fuchs, 1995; Johnson, 1981; Kaflus, 1984; Konner, 1976; Mugney & Doise, 1978; Piaget, 1926; Richards, King, & Joseph, 2003; Slavin, 1993; Viadero, 2003; Vygotsky, 1978; Walberg, 1998	As the teacher models ways children can work together and tutor one another, the quantity and quality of the social interactions between the children will improve and increase.	Intervention one: Beginning sound game. Students were given picture cards and were to match them to the card on the chart that had the same beginning sound. Intervention two: Children recited the nursery rhyme Hey Diddle Diddle, then put rhyme or order-and-match sentence strips to the pictures. Intervention three: Letter cube game. One student rolled the letter cube and stated the sound that appeared. The other student wrote this on the board. After three rolls the child decided if it was a meaningful word.

(*continued*)

Table 8.1. *(continued)*

Observations	Postintervention Findings	Implications	Reflections
The number of positive peer tutoring strategies/behaviors children exhibited increased. The children are much more aware of the need to provide assistance. The children also internalized the strategies and transferred them to other activities in the classroom by helping their buddies perform various tasks. The social climate of the classroom improved.	The number of positive peer teaching behaviors exhibited by the children increased dramatically from the baseline to intervention one. The number dropped during the next three interventions, yet the children still exhibited more positive behaviors than at the beginning. Among these positive behaviors were children needing help asking for help from their peers and an increase in the number of times children provided verbal instruction.	Pair children with others instead of their buddies.	The research yielded positive results, and therefore it is worthwhile to continue building on this beginning and expanding the project to compare children's interactions in a structured activity as opposed to one that was of the children's choosing, and to develop more ways of pairing the children.

Direction for New Cycle of Action Research

Questions for future research: How did the use of peer tutoring aid in prejudice reduction based on learning ability? Can this procedure be carried on from one grade to another? Can children transfer behaviors learned from one classroom back to their homerooms? Could peer tutoring be successful with larger class sizes?

pocket chart, which held cards showing the letter of the alphabet and a picture that began with that letter. The children were to place the picture cards under the letter that began with the appropriate sound. Mrs. A gave the children directions as a group. She called each pair up, handed one of the children the cards, and told them they must work together to complete the task. She also told them to pretend she was not there and that she would be writing about what they were doing. She did not provide any modeling regarding how she wanted the children to complete the task.

She observed the children interacting to perform the task and took anecdotal notes of the interaction that occurred between each pair of children. As she read back through the notes, she placed tally marks under the appropriate column on a checklist when a child performed one of the behaviors she was looking for. She also wrote an explanation of the behavior under the appropriate indicator. She transferred this data to a chart. As she completed the checklist and chart, she noticed that the children exhibited behaviors not on the checklist. Therefore, Mrs. A expanded the number of indicators to make the checklist more specific. She went back through the anecdotal notes and completed the revised checklist. Once the revised checklist had been completed for each pair of children, she transferred the data to a chart, which had also been revised.

The data sheets charting the interactions provided a clear picture of the types of interactions that occurred. Her general findings, after completing the baseline assessment, were that the children did not have a great deal of trouble sharing the materials or working together side by side. Yet the type of interaction that occurred was parallel in nature. There was not a great deal of conversation as the children worked on the task. Some of the children helped or corrected their partners, but there was no explanation of why the card was in the wrong place or why it was moved. Mrs. A believed that as she modeled ways the children could work with their partners, the degree that children interact with one another would increase.

Mrs. A, therefore, saw the possibilities in implementing a program based on peer tutoring and positive interdependence to create a classroom atmosphere where children were encouraged to share, support, and help one another. This, she hoped, would then build community and respect for one another.

Based on this information about her students, Mrs. A decided to develop her research based on how the use of peer tutoring and positive interdependence affect social interaction among children. By modeling the way children could work together and tutor each other, she reasoned that the quantity and quality of the social interactions would improve.

Step 3: Design an Intervention

Mrs. A selected two classes that she taught to implement peer tutoring practices. There were six children in each class. A child with a high ability level was paired with a child who had a lower ability level. The pairs were mixed by race and gender, and they were called "buddies."

Mrs. A developed an initial checklist that addressed the following areas of interaction: positive comments, negative comments, helped or corrected a partner, explained why help or correction was given, questioned a partner or asked a partner for help, and took turns. This checklist was used to determine the baseline of social interaction in her classroom. She soon found that this list was too general and did not yield the kind of data she had expected. Mrs. A found that the list did not differentiate between a child correcting another's error and simply providing the other child with assistance. Therefore, the teacher had to go back and review the literature relating to peer tutoring in order to revise the checklist of behaviors she specifically wanted to model and observe in the children.

Once Mrs. A had again clarified her own expectations for the development of positive, open communication and support between buddies, she was able to revise the checklist to focus on and incorporate ways that children could express their needs as well as ways the children could provide help to one another. She wanted the checklist to reflect how each child helped the other, not by completing the task for his or her buddy but by explaining the reasoning behind the action he or she did for the buddy. Basically, could the children show other children what to do instead of simply doing it for them? Her revised checklist addressed the following concerns:

- Asked partner for help
- Provided assistance to partner

- Provided verbal instruction while assisting partner
- Corrected partner's errors
- Corrected partner's errors with an explanation
- Provided positive comments or praise

Mrs. A also developed a checklist to critique the modeling she would perform. She hoped this modeling would encourage the children to use peer-tutoring strategies. The modeling critique checklist drawn up by the teacher included the same areas of concern an observer would look for when evaluating the children. Her colleague or another observer would rate her modeling as very effective, somewhat effective, or ineffective. The checklist would also include questions that elicited reflections from the observer on the modeling session. These questions related to whether or not the teacher had modeled ways the children could perform each of the areas of concern. Questions relating to whether or not the observer felt the children grasped the concept were posed, as well as questions asking for suggestions for improving the modeling and checklist. The observer was asked his or her general impression of the interventions that took place and if he or she could see growth in the children from one intervention to the next.

The rationale for both of the checklists mentioned is that the two served as a guideline for the behaviors the teacher wished to observe. Each checklist identified points or areas of concern she wanted to model and observe in the children. Mrs. A's colleagues were given both checklists before they observed the children. The expectation was that the observer would use each checklist and write anecdotal notes as well.

Step 4: Implement the Intervention

The first activity was a modeling session by Mrs. A. The children responded positively to this session, which is evident in the way the total number of positive behaviors rose dramatically. During the second and third activities, the teacher found that she had selected activities that were too easily completed by the students without assistance. Therefore, she and her colleagues were unable to obtain any in-depth data that would reveal areas in which students needed to further develop skills. With these new and important observations on hold, the teacher then developed activities that were more on the children's instructional level, as opposed to their independent work level.

Step 5: Collect Data from the Results of the Intervention

Mrs. A used several sources of data: her own observations, observations from colleagues, and two checklists to be used by her colleagues—one to record children's behaviors and the other to note the teacher's effective modeling practices. Figures 8.1 and 8.2 show how the teacher organized her checklists.

Step 6: Evaluate and Assess the Effectiveness of the Intervention

Overall the number of positive peer-tutoring strategies exhibited by the children increased. The increase was very dramatic between the baseline assessment and the first intervention. The number of strategies implemented increased from the baseline and the second and third intervention, but the increase was not as dramatic as between the baseline and the first intervention. The reason for this was that the activities were more open-ended, and the children also did not require as much assistance to complete these activities.

The quantitative aspect of the findings does not paint an accurate picture of the quality of the interactions that took place. The children seemed to internalize the strategies. This was evident when the children began to log onto the computer. They informed the teacher that they were not sitting with their buddies. They then asked their buddies for help. Some of the children monitored their partners and provided assistance without being asked. The children provided some verbal instruction to their partners, but not necessarily enough or the right kind of instruction. The teacher noted that this would need to be the next area of research (i.e., how to teach children to respond in a variety of appropriate ways to their partners who are asking for help).

Mrs. A noted one important finding regarding the children with a higher ability level. This group appeared to grasp the concept of positive interdependence more easily than their counterparts of lower

Name of Student	Positive Comments	Negative Comments	Helped or Corrected Partner	Explained Why Help or Correction Was Given	Questioned Partner or Asked Partner for Help	Took Turns

Comments:

Figure 8.1. Student Checklist (to Be Used by Observers)

How effectively were the following behaviors modeled? Please provide examples and explanations.

	Very Effective	Somewhat Effective	Ineffective
Ways children can ask for help			
Ways children can help each other			
Verbal instruction and correction			
Explanation of instruction and correction			
Ways to provide praise			

Were the above behaviors easily identified?

Do you feel that the children grasped the concept? Explain.

Do you have any suggestions for improving the modeling?

Do you have any suggestions for improving the checklists?

What was your general impression of the observation and the intervention that took place?

Can you see growth in the children?

Figure 8.2. Checklist for the Teacher

ability. She comments that there could be several reasons for this. One would be that the children of lower ability were never providing the help, but always receiving it.

Step 7: Reflect on the Implications of the Intervention

Mrs. A noted that the concept of having a buddy was very interesting for the children. Each child could recall who his or her buddy was. As she began the mini-lesson to model positive ways the children could work together, the children were attentive. Each child was able to provide examples of ways to ask his or her buddy for help. She stressed the need for the children to explain their actions or the help they gave their buddies instead of just completing the task for them. The children were also asked to reflect on the modeling session. Mrs. A was very pleased with the way the children were able to recall the information presented. Upon reviewing the data obtained from this observation, the teacher was able to gain several insights. When the students with a high ability level provided help, an explanation accompanied the help. The higher-ability students also did not require help to complete the task. Therefore, the lower-ability students were not provided the opportunity to tutor. This caused Mrs. A to reflect further about the possibilities of pairing two lower-ability children.

Step 8: Reflect on the Overall Process

As a result of conducting this action research, Mrs. A planned on continuing this project with the same group of children in order to further their development of positive social interaction that was begun in the first phase of the project. She also decided to expand the concept of the project and compare children's interactions in a structured activity as opposed to one that is a choice made by the children, as well as pair the children with other students in the room to take into consideration further diverse pairings. As a result of this teacher's research, several other teachers began implementing some of the same strategies for their students.

Step 9: Begin the Cycle Again by Identifying a New or Continuing Area of Concern

Mrs. A ended this cycle of her action research with more questions than answers. This shows the efficacy of this process in that it produces high levels of reflective and critical thinking about one's teaching practice. Among her questions to be approached in the next cycle of research are the following: Can this be carried from one classroom to another? How can the use of peer tutoring aid in prejudice reduction based on learning ability?

REFERENCES

Brownell, C. A., & Carriger, M. S. (1990). Changes in cooperation and self–other differentiation during the second year. *Child Development, 6,* 1164–1174.

Cohen, P. A., Kulik, J. A., & Kulik, C. C. (1982). Educational outcomes of tutoring: A meta-analysis of findings. *American Educational Research Journal, 19,* 237–248.

Delquadri, J., Greenwood, D. R., Whorton, D., Carta, J. J., & Hall, R. V. (1986). Classwide peer tutoring. *Exceptional Children, 52,* 535–542.

Foot, H., & Howe, C. (1998). The psycho-educational basis of peer-assisted learning. In L. Topping & S. Ehly (Eds.), *Peer-assisted learning* (pp. 27–43). Hillsdale, NJ: Erlbaum.

Franca, V. M., Kerr, M. M., Reitz, A. K., & Lambert, D. (1990). Peer tutoring among behaviorally disordered students: Academic and social benefits to tutor and tutee. *Education and Treatment of Children, 13,* 109–128.

Fuchs, D., Fuchs, L., & Burish, P. (2000). Peer-assisted learning strategies: An evidence-based practice to promote reading achievement. *Learning Disabilities Research and Practice, 15*(2), 85–91.

Fuchs, D., Mathes, P. C., & Fuchs, L. S. (1995). *Peabody peer-assisted learning strategies (PALS): Reading methods.* Nashville, TN: Peabody College, Vanderbilt University.

Johnson, D. W. (1981). Student–student interaction: The neglected variable in education. *Educational Researcher, 10,* 5–10.

Kaflus, G. R. (1984). Peer-mediated intervention: A critical review. *Child and Family Behavior Therapy, 6,* 17–43.

Konner, M. (1976). Relations among infants and juveniles in comparative perspective. *Social Science Information, 15,* 371–402.

Mugny, G., & Doise, W. (1978). Socio-cognitive conflict and structure of individual and cognitive performances. *European Journal of Social Psychology, 8,* 181–192.

Piaget, J. (1926). *The language and thought of the child.* NY: Harcourt, Brace and World.

Richards, P., King, S., & Joseph, J. (2003). PALS at Mooloolah State School: A class-wide peer-tutoring program. *Primary & Middle Years Educator, 1*(1), 25–28.

Slavin, R (1983). *Cooperative learning.* NY: Longman.

Viadero, D. (2003). Studies show peer tutoring yields benefits for students. *Education Week, 22*(2), 5.

Vygotsky, L. S. (1978). *Thought and language.* NY: Wiley.

Walberg, H. J. (1998). Forward. In L. Topping & S. Ehly (Eds.), *Peer-assisted learning* (pp. 27–43). Hillsdale, NJ: Erlbaum.

CHAPTER 9

Cooperative Groups

It has been found that when conflict is managed constructively, there are many positive outcomes on the part of students, such as increased energy, curiosity, and motivation; increased achievement, retention, insight, creativity, problem solving, and synthesis; increased healthy cognitive and social development; and a strengthening of relationships (Johnson & Johnson, 1998).

There are five essential elements to cooperative learning activities: positive interdependence, face-to-face promotive interaction, individual and group accountability, interpersonal and small-group skills, and group processing (Johnson, Johnson, & Holubec, 1994). Positive interdependence is the linking of students in a way that they cannot succeed unless everyone succeeds. Face-to-face promotive interaction occurs when students are engaged in a collaborative activity that forces them to share resources, help and support one another, and encourage and applaud one another's efforts in a real-work situation where the students are face to face. The third element, individual and group accountability, means that both the group and the individual are accountable for contributing their fair share to the work of the group. Through group work, individual competency should be strengthened. Interpersonal and small-group skills, the fourth element, involve both taskwork and teamwork. The social skills needed to create successful taskwork and teamwork must be modeled and taught by the teacher. The social skills that should emerge will be leadership, decision making, trust building, communication, and conflict management. The last element, group processing, is defined as group members discussing how well they are achieving goals and maintaining effective working relationships. With time, the students should be able to communicate effectively, provide leadership, make decisions, and understand one another's perspectives. Systematic use of cooperative learning can promote the development of caring and committed relationships for all children (Johnson & Johnson, 1998).

COOPERATIVE LEARNING GROUPS CASE STUDY

The following case study describes one first grade teacher's attempts to foster tolerant behavior in her students (see table 9.1). Mrs. F decided to use cooperative learning groups with her students in an attempt to increase cooperation, respect, and tolerance for one another. She had used cooperative grouping in the past but found that by being bound by an action research process, she didn't give up when the going got rough.

Step 1: Identify the Concern

The experienced teacher had taught for twenty years. During that time, Mrs. F had used a number of motivational tools to push or pull her children along. The games, contests, stickers, hugs, words of praise, written messages, and so on all had one common thread. The collective focus of these rewards was to get each child to enjoy success. She wanted this feeling of success to be so pleasant and rewarding that they would take over the seeking of this feeling for themselves. She also hoped that a joy of learning would be its own reward.

Mrs. F had used competitive games and contests many times in her classroom but found they worked well with only a certain type of child, those who were bright and confident and who had experienced the most success. But these are the children who need the least pushing. Occasionally she found that the less able child persisted and won, but usually this was not the case.

After some critical and reflective thinking, Mrs. F began to think about the "I win, you lose" mentality and how she had overlooked the discord these competitive activities had brought to her classroom over the years. She also wondered if children had just changed and become more blatant about flaunting their superiority. She felt dissatisfied with the results of competitive games, did not like the antagonism they

Table 9.1. Cooperative Groups

Problem	Research	Hypothesis/Baseline	Intervention
Students today are very intolerant of one another. Many of the activities used in schools do nothing to increase cooperation, respect, and tolerance for other individuals.	Johnson & Johnson, 1998; Johnson, Johnson, & Holubec, 1994; Lindauer & Petrie, 1997	Cooperative learning activities will promote tolerant and empathetic behavior among children. Attitude surveys: Students were surveyed to determine how they feel they are accepted by their friends. They were also surveyed to determine how they feel toward their friends. These same surveys were administered again at the end of the research period.	Social skills are taught to the children. Positive and negative behaviors for successful cooperative group work are discussed and listed. Cooperative learning groups work together.

Observations	Postintervention Findings	Implications	Reflections
Checklists were used at each observation to record the number of tolerant or intolerant behaviors identified during the cooperative learning activity. Reflections were written after each observation and again at the end of the entire project.	Comparisons of the baseline survey and the postintervention survey. Comparisons of the results of the checklists. Conclusions reached about cooperative learning as determined from the reflections and discussion among the team.	The cooperative learning activities were often loud with quite a lot of intolerant behavior. However, a growth in tolerant behavior was also observed.	The research reflects the development of cooperative learning skills. The teacher recognizes cooperative learning as a valuable teaching tool. Cooperative learning challenges the children in a number of ways, academically, emotionally, and socially.

Direction for New Cycle of Action Research

Continue to develop new learning activities to get at intolerant behavior. Develop new observation checklists to zero in on tolerant behaviors.

brought, and saw resentment and anger replace good sportsmanship and gracious behavior.

Therefore, Mrs. F decided to target the development of more caring and respectful attitudes in the children toward one another. She wanted to find a teaching method or make changes to her classroom that would promote the creation of a caring community of learners.

Step 2: Collect Information about the Concern

Once she had identified the problem as the children's negative behaviors, the teacher searched for an appropriate teaching method to initiate in her classroom. She decided that the approach must encourage a classroom atmosphere that was kinder and friendlier. She wanted to build a spirit of cooperation in place of the competitive attitudes she now found. She wanted to see the least able child embraced and nurtured by others who were stronger and more confident. While she definitely wanted to remove the competitive activities she had used in the past, she felt this would be only a beginning since the students did not know how to help one another, nor had they developed attitudes toward one another that were rooted in respect and a desire to help.

The research gathered by Mrs. F and her team of undergraduates seemed to indicate that cooperative learning might prove to be a useful strategy in turning around her classroom. Its outcomes included improved academic achievement, the development of social skills, and improved student attitudes about school and peers (Lindauer & Petrie, 1997). The team felt the following points were key to understanding how to implement this project:

- The project must include activities with positive interdependence.
- The students must be put in situations where they need to share resources, support one another, and encourage one another.
- The project must include activities that would require both individual and group accountability.
- Through collaborative taskwork, students would practice teamwork.
- Teamwork skills that need to be modeled by the teacher included effective communication, decision making, trust building, and conflict management.

- The project should help students become caring and respectful of one another.
- Cautions: Not all students learn best by working together in groups since there might be conflicts within the group. Therefore, social skills should be taught before, during, and after cooperative learning activities.

The team then decided on the final question for their research: "When cooperative activities are implemented in the classroom, will the children develop more tolerance and empathy toward one another?"

To determine if cooperative learning activities would make a difference in her students' tolerant and empathetic behavior, Mrs. F developed an instrument to record the children's attitudes toward one another and reveal tolerant and intolerant attitudes. This instrument would provide a baseline to which future information would be compared. Mrs. F developed a "friendship attitude survey," a series of written statements that allowed the children to express how they felt their friends regarded them and how they regarded their friends (see figure 9.1). The first part of the survey consisted of seven statements that gave evidence of how the children interacted with their friends. They could chose "never," "sometimes," or "always." The second part also consisted of seven statements giving evidence of how the children perceived their friends felt about them. Students were given the same options as in the first part in answering each statement. Each statement was read aloud, and students were given an appropriate amount of time to check one box. As is necessary with first graders, Mrs. F let them know that all answers were correct since it was the child's opinion. Even with this instruction, the teacher felt some students were marking what they assumed the teacher wanted or what they assumed was the "correct" answer. She felt that this instrument needed more field trials before it would yield more accurate results.

Step 3: Design an Intervention

In planning her intervention, Mrs. F first engaged in critical and reflective thinking about her project. In realizing that the objectives of cooperative learning activities were far surpassed by the very basic

I take turns with my friends.	Never	Sometimes	Always
I listen to my friends.	Never	Sometimes	Always
I tell my friends when they do well.	Never	Sometimes	Always
I ask my friends to play.	Never	Sometimes	Always
I share with my friends.	Never	Sometimes	Always
If my friends are sad, I try to make them feel better.	Never	Sometimes	Always
I help my friends when they need help.	Never	Sometimes	Always
My friends take turns with me.	Never	Sometimes	Always
My friends listen to me.	Never	Sometimes	Always
My friends tell me to do well.	Never	Sometimes	Always
My friends ask me to play.	Never	Sometimes	Always
My friends share with me.	Never	Sometimes	Always
My friends want me on their team.	Never	Sometimes	Always
My friends help me if I need help.	Never	Sometimes	Always

Figure 9.1. Surveys of Children's Attitudes

goal of a group of students completing a task together, the teacher began to organize her intervention around the five basic elements the team had discovered during the research phase. She began to focus on certain aspects of cooperative learning that she felt needed to be tackled first. The first circumstance she recognized is that children do not necessarily have the social skills necessary for working in groups; therefore, time must be taken prior to and during cooperative learning activities to teach these social skills. She also realized she would need to use the concept of interdependence and that groups needed to be mixed and diverse in gender, race, and academic strength, which would provide the opportunity for students who might not have previously interacted with one another to become friends. She also realized, as indicated by the research, that members of the group should assume or be assigned different roles such as recorder, leader, person who communicates with the teacher, person who gets the supplies, and so on. This would also lessen conflict in the group. As Mrs. F continued to read about cooperative grouping, she recognized the need for her role to change as well. The students would take on the major role of thinking critically and problem solving, instead of the teacher doing it for the students. While this new role of mentor, or guide, is not less demanding, it does change the flow of information acquisition. In lecture-type classes, students must sit through and listen to a great deal of information they already know, whereas the cooperative groups allow for self-pacing and include the teacher only when the group is unable to solve its own problems.

Step 4: Implement the Intervention

The children began the cooperative learning activity with little prior knowledge or experience of working in a sharing and helpful manner. Most of the work Mrs. F had done in her classroom that year had been large group and teacher directed. Individual work had also been required, but this had also been guided and supervised by the teacher. In addition, the children had been involved with activities of combined play, helping one another with words, and small unstructured projects. This was the first cooperative activity she had planned for her children that year.

Before each cooperative learning activity, Mrs. F asked students to talk about what good and bad behaviors were and list them on the chalkboard. On the good side, the list usually included talking quietly, discussing, taking turns, voting, and saying nice things to one another. On the bad side, the list usually included talking too loud, arguing, being bossy, and saying mean things to one another.

Mrs. F explained to the children that they would practice sorting coins, constructing a chart, and writing three questions about their chart. The children had quite a bit of previous experience with charts, graphs, and diagrams, along with practice in writing questions about graphs. The new element in this activity would be working together cooperatively to complete the tasks.

Before they began the actual work, Mrs. F explained to the children the plan of working together to construct the chart. She called on several students to define what cooperation meant to them. One little boy immediately volunteered, "It means to agree." Other children joined in, contributing their ideas about working together. She then introduced the word *compromise* and gave examples of how, why, and when it is used. The teacher then explained the task of sorting coins and gluing them onto a grid. After this, they could make up three questions about the money. She gave the children four rules to follow: (1) Everyone gets a turn at the basic task of sorting and gluing the coins, (2) the glue would be shared, (3) everyone should contribute to composing the questions, and (4) one or more of them could write the questions.

After clearing a space in the classroom for the children to be able to work together in groups, Mrs. F selected who would be in which group. As expected, there was a lot of wrangling over the coins, which had been given to the children on a sheet of cardboard. Once they were able to sort the coins, not necessarily to everyone's satisfaction, the students began the task of arranging them on the grid. Again there was much complaining and changing as they finally settled on their arrangements. The teacher, in the role of mentor, moved around the room offering encouragement, urging students to talk within their groups to reach decisions, but trying not to settle any disputes. Children who felt they were not being treated fairly turned to the teacher to force the others to settle disputes. After having developed the children's view of the world as teacher driven, to not interfere was very hard. To create interdependence, she made them share one tube of glue, which revealed a lack of patience in some students and courtesy in others. In the groups, instead of democratically going about choosing those to write questions, children volunteered and the others went along with it.

The second cooperative learning activity attempted was a construction project related to a story in reading. The children had been reading *The Surprise Family*, and the day began with a rereading of the story and a discussion of the story elements. After reading, Mrs. F told the children they would be making an animal out of a large piece of construction paper. This animal would be their "surprise animal." While the teacher demonstrated how to cut out the various shapes and assemble an animal, she didn't tell them they would be taking parts of several different animals to make up one whole new animal.

After the children had the parts laid out on their desks, Mrs. F let them know about her surprise. She asked them to recall the story where the author had tricked his readers. They remembered the story with amusement. She then explained that she had tricked them. What she wanted them to do was not make their own animals, but make a group animal. She explained that they would be taking parts from each of their animals and putting these parts together with other children in the group to make an animal that would truly be a surprise. The reception to this idea was mixed.

As she did each time before the children were to do cooperative work, they went through the list of good and bad behaviors and listed them on the board, they discussed how to work successfully in cooperative groups, they moved their desks to make room to work on the floor, the teacher assigned groups which were different from the day before, and the children began work.

The children worked on the floor. Each one carried the pieces to the work area. Some children immediately had ideas about what they could do. These ideas very often used all their pieces and very few of anyone else's. There was talking, arguing, beating on the floor, complaining, and even some cooperation. The teacher moved around the room offering suggestions such as, "What does the whole group think about this?" and "Do you like the feet?"

In one activity the teacher reviewed the role-play she had helped model the day before. The idea was to review the role-play to identify why some behaviors work and others don't. Mrs. F started, "Five children wanted to paint a doghouse different colors. Two wanted blue and the other three wanted red, yellow, and pink. They argued and argued, getting nowhere. Was this behavior productive? *No.* What could they do? *Take turns telling why they think their color is the best.* Yes, and the result of this was that one of the children who wanted the doghouse to be yellow was convinced by the ones who wanted the doghouse blue that blue was the best color. *Discussion may lead to someone changing his or her way of thinking.* The other two children would not change. What can be done? *There are three who want blue. This is more. It should be blue. Majority rules.* Now the girl who wanted pink begins to pout. What can we do to make her feel better? *We will try to let her have her way in something else. We can say something good to her. She and the other little boy can paint a rainbow on the side of the doghouse using their colors. Compromise. Everybody wins!*" The children had remembered the activity very well.

Step 5: Collect Data from the Results of the Intervention

The results of the project were determined by analyzing data from several sources: student surveys, observation checklists, the observers' reflections, and the teacher's own reflections. In reviewing the data from the observation checklist, as expected, the first observation revealed quite a lot of intolerant behaviors and less tolerant behaviors. The students had not had a great deal of experience with cooperative learning activities. Of course, with the implementation of intervention strategies and experience with cooperative learning activities, one would expect to see a decline in the intolerant behaviors and an increase in tolerant behaviors. However, as the project proceeded, it became evident that the tolerant behaviors were not replacing the intolerant. At the end of each visit, the observers turned in checklists with a majority of intolerant behaviors recorded.

When the data from the checklists were finally arranged in the form of a graph, a clearer picture of what had transpired was revealed. Yes, the intolerant behavior never did decline; in fact, there was a slight increase during the project. In the last team meeting, the research team members discussed their perceptions as to why the intolerant behaviors were being recorded so much more. Participants had noted in their reflections that, in their opinion, the children had made progress in cooperative behaviors. As the leader of the team, the teacher observed that because intolerant behavior is so compelling and attention grabbing, it is easy to overlook cooperative behavior when uncooperative behavior is going on right next to it. Consider this: If an inexperienced observer was watching four groups of children, some exhibiting tolerant and some intolerant behavior, would the observer be more likely to notice the group quietly passing the glue or someone in another group saying despicably, "I hate you"? It is very easy to see only the loud, dramatic behaviors. Also, with a change from teacher-centered processes to cooperative learning activities, the children were interacting more, thus increasing levels of all types of active behaviors.

Recognizing this fact, Mrs. F refocused on this graph and for the first time noticed that the goal of increasing tolerant behavior had been accomplished in the project. The increase in tolerant behaviors was greater than the increase of the intolerant behaviors. Ideally one would also want to see a decrease in intolerant behaviors as well, but perhaps a research project conducted for a greater length of time may show these results. Most studies that were cited in the literature lasted much longer than this study.

A compelling piece of evidence developed at the end of the project. The completion of the postintervention surveys provided more support for the previous findings. The "friendship attitude survey" had been given at the beginning of the project. It was presented in two parts, the "I" sheet and the "My Friends" sheet. In comparing pre- and postintervention survey data, it is evident that all children improved how they felt about their friends and especially their perception of how their friends felt about them.

Step 6: Evaluate and Assess the Effectiveness of the Intervention

In discussing the coin sorting activity later with her team, they all noted the same changes that occurred in the groups. Group A started off in a fairly cooperative manner. The students launched their work quickly, yet as they entered deeper into the project, their cohesion fell apart. They began disputing and quarreling more than working together. Consequently, their product was not as well done and took longer to complete. Group B started off very productively but could not agree on how the coins would be divided, how they would be arranged, and so on. However, after the children got deeper into the project, they began to work together better. This group finally created quite a good product and worked in a reasonably cooperative manner. Group C fell somewhere in the middle of the other two groups.

This coin sorting activity was very noisy. Mrs. F felt that since these students were grouped cooperatively only during less structured recess-type activities, the students saw this as not a serious academic activity and thought it was okay to be loud. She also noticed that, on a positive note, the children seemed to take a very active interest in being part of a group and desired to contribute to the creation of a product.

During the second day, when Mrs. F had the students assemble a new animal, she made the following observations. Group A appeared to get off to a reasonably good start. One would have predicted that they would finish first with the best project. This was not the case. Their cooperative spirit dissolved into bickering and squabbling. They were jealous and petty. Group B began with little agreement among them but was able to gradually work together quite well. Group C had only one girl. The boys tried to dominate this group and force her to name her animal after a wrestler.

Again, this activity was very noisy. The children were enthusiastic and loud. Mrs. F was pleased to note that one of her students who was not high achieving took a very active role in constructing the surprise animal. He directed others, expressed his opinions, and argued for his ideas, things he would not normally do in the regular classroom environment.

Mrs. F also noted that she now had time to observe her students, even though she was still facilitating the learning process. Being able to watch closely and focus on particular students intently eases the teacher's job of planning for instruction, since she now is able to spend more time noting children's work habits.

After many more interventions, Mrs. F began seeing that group effort was producing better work from the students. In particular, a reading lesson required more discussion and sharing of what each other thought. This meant the students were beginning to identify strategies that were helpful to group work. Mrs. F began to write down the strategies the children were adopting so she could continue to build more successful cooperative group activities.

Step 7: Reflect on the Implications of the Intervention

Mrs. F began the project excited but doubtful about using cooperative groups in her classroom. Like most teachers, she had tried grouping children to work together on different assignments and projects in the past—without much success. She realized, in hindsight, that she had never stayed with cooperative learning long enough to allow the children to learn how to do it. Another mistake she had made, and was sure that most teachers make, was that she assumed children knew cooperative behavior. This is probably one of the major misconceptions made by educators in implementing group learning. Children must be taught how to work together. This is especially true of today's students since they live in a society that glorifies violence and winning. Many come from homes where scrapping and fighting are part of everyday life. These are the children who tell the teacher, when challenged about a playground dispute, "My mother told me if anybody hits you or bothers you, you hit them back." These are not fertile grounds to plant the seeds of tolerance and empathy. However, this is a seed that needs to be sown and nurtured. It falls to the school to show these children another way of dealing with life's conflicts.

As detrimental as assuming the children know their roles is assuming the teacher knows his or her role. A teacher whose normal teaching style is lecturing will probably resist cooperative learning. After the initial instruction, the teacher steps back and lets the children take over the lesson. Through discussion, explaining, demonstrating, experimenting, and even arguing, the children discover what works and what doesn't. The teacher who assumes that this frees him or her to go to the desk and grade papers is dooming the cooperative activities to failure. The teacher is not freed from involvement in the class. The involvement merely takes on a different role: from lecturer to guide, demonstrator to audience, and performer to cheerleader. The spotlight shifts from the teacher to the students. But if the teacher shrugs off any of these new roles, the children lose interest and direction and the academic activity dissolves into playtime.

The focus of this project was to increase tolerance and empathy. As the team progressed through the project, Mrs. F was increasingly disappointed to see the observers continually turn in their checklists with the majority of recorded items as intolerant. She resigned herself to disproving most of the positive claims that have been made about cooperative learning. It was not until she converted the data from the checklists into graph form that she could see that she had in fact successfully proven the hypothesis: "When cooperative learning methods are used in the classroom, the children will develop tolerance and empathy for one another."

In reflecting about the still-high rate of intolerant behavior, the teacher could only speculate. Perhaps the intolerant behaviors were easier for the undergraduate and less-experienced observers to pick out since they were loud, eye catching, and disruptive. Tolerant behaviors, on the other hand, are usually quiet and not attention grabbing.

Another element of this project that may bear looking at is the variety of different activities Mrs. F had her children do for the observed periods. There were construction projects, reading, worksheets, and games. Mrs. F suspected that the type of activity might also have had some bearing on the number of recorded tolerant and intolerant behaviors.

Step 8: Reflect on the Overall Process

Mrs. F found that her role as a teacher changed as she began doing the cooperative activities. She had always spent time demonstrating and lecturing to the class, which she felt gave her children lots of opportunities for discovery learning. But once she began the cooperative learning activities, she realized that many more children at the same time were discovering, explaining, and learning. Before, she would have six or seven children watching a lesson with five or six daydreaming. Now she had everyone participating. Those children who in the past had been passively attending the class were now engaged and demonstrating active behaviors, both good and bad. Now Mrs. F had to work with the behaviors of all of her students, not just the four or five who, in the past, were attending to her teacher-centered lessons.

Step 9: Begin the Cycle Again by Identifying a New or Continuing Area of Concern

Mrs. F decided that when she started this project again the following year she would revise the checklist and consider recording just tolerant behaviors. Another change she would make would be to ask each observer to focus on only one child, recording the various types of tolerant and intolerant behaviors. This would allow the observers to stay with one situation and hopefully stop being distracted from one group to another by disruptive and intolerant behavior. An improvement in one or two targeted children would provide a sampling of what may be happening in the room. The observer could also record the strategies these children were picking up and utilizing over and over. This, in turn, would help the teacher plan further intervention strategies.

Mrs. F felt, in the short time she experimented with cooperative learning, that the benefits to children's improved deportment as well as their achievement were reasons enough to continue not only using this process but also embedding it into her teaching practice. This first cycle of experimenting with action research convinced her more than ever that this reflective process not only was valuable, but it also opened doors to thinking in new ways.

REFERENCES

Johnson, D., & Johnson, R. (1998). Promoting safe educational and community environments: The three Cs program. In A. Reynolds, R. Weissberg, & H. Walberg, (Eds.), *Positive outcomes in children and youth: Promotion and evaluation.* Chicago: University of Illinois.

Johnson, D., Johnson, R., Holubec, E. (1994). *The new circles of learning: Cooperation in the classroom and school.* Alexandria, VA: Association for Supervision and Curriculum Development.

Lindauer, P., & Petrie, G. (1997). A review of cooperative learning: An alternative to everyday instructional strategies. *Journal of Instructional Psychology, 24*(3), 183–187.

CHAPTER 10

Parent–Child–Community Collaboration

Research has shown that key components for success in at-risk youths involve an attachment to a caring adult, the acquisition of social skills to deal with peer influences, attendance at an effective school, residence in a safe community, and exposure to career paths (Taylor & Dryfoos, 1998). If children lack some or all of these interconnected support systems, they will be less likely to become fully functioning and contributing adults in society. Increasingly, schools are forming partnerships with parents and community groups to mobilize additional resources to deal with these problems. Programs that have been successful have recognized the importance of using existing family and community assets; enhancing and supporting the cultural dynamics and professional relationships within families and the community; identifying the qualities of resiliency in children; illustrating the cycles that children move through as they develop; and developing a program philosophy (Townsel, 1997). The relationships that families have with people in the community help create competent children, and the elders of the community provide the glue to bring school and community together. "The matriarch has historically been at the forefront of the family–school partnership, yet these women are noticeably absent from most mentoring programs" (Townsel, 1997).

The focus at school is usually on academics, where the child is viewed in terms of lowered expectations, when in fact, the focus should be on the child's resiliency. It has been found that children with resilience are able to endure; they continue to come to school despite school failure. Resilient children often build a skill or talent in a certain area and are able to establish significant relationships despite past difficulties (Wolin & Wolin, 1993). Models such as Big Brother/Big Sister build on the existing assets that children bring to the relationship.

Older people are in an ideal position to provide support for the kind of mentoring needed for these at-risk youths. Older people are usually retired, and because of their interest in volunteering, they are able to give the time, attention, patience, and understanding needed to improve the lives of these children. For children who feel their futures are clouded, an older person can offer life perspectives for the children, perspectives that are rooted in resilience and survival and that can provide the continuity between past, present, and future (Freedman, 1988).

PARENT–CHILD–COMMUNITY COLLABORATION CASE STUDY

The teacher in this case study reached out to the community to try to meet the needs of her children who were living in poverty, often violent toward one another, and showing disrespect for elders (see table 10.1).

Step 1: Identify the Concern

This fifth grade teacher had taught for many years at a neighborhood school in an impoverished area of the city. Recently, the school district had decided to close this school and build a new school in another neighborhood; the children would be transferred to three schools, busing about one-third to the new school. Mrs. T was one of the teachers transferred from the old neighborhood school to the new school and thought that with all the wonderful new resources available, she would have a very positive and effective year of teaching. In looking over the data on the children from the previous year, though, she realized that she may not have as easy a year as she had expected. The students who were being bused in from the low socioeconomic neighborhood where she had previously taught were in the bottom third of her class in terms of academic achievement. Their reading and math skills were very low. They had also been in numerous scuffles and fights with classmates.

Table 10.1. Parent–Child–Community Collaboration

Problem	Research	Hypothesis/Baseline	Intervention
The closing of the old neighborhood school left children, already fragile from poverty and neighborhood violence, more vulnerable.	Freedman, 1988; Taylor & Dryfoos, 1998; Townsel, 1997; Wolin & Wolin, 1993	If children are paired with seniors from their community through an intergenerational project, conflict will occur less frequently during school activities and children's achievement will improve.	After-school meetings two days per week of paired seniors and children. Activities include reading skills, life skills, and social skills.

Observations	Postintervention Findings	Implications	Reflections
Teacher College supervisor	Postintervention data found significant gains in all three areas targeted, but the most gains were made in life and social skills. Both seniors and children reported improved interactions with children's peers. The teacher noted a drop in number of discipline referrals and some improvement in reading skills.	The family resource center provided a positive support system and an extended family atmosphere that created success for children.	The action research process provided positive outcomes for a difficult situation. The success from this first try encouraged the teacher to build a more permanent process the next year.

Direction for New Cycle of Action Research

The teacher felt that parents played a minimal role in this research, yet she felt they were a vital component to creating success for their children. Parent involvement would close the school–community–parent circle. The next cycle of research should include opportunities for parents to participate without further stress, develop links with other community-based organizations, and provide more ways to recognize the important work seniors are doing.

Step 2: Collect Information about the Concern

When the elementary school in the impoverished neighborhood closed, more than 90 percent of the students were already on free or reduced lunches. Before the facility closed, children were able to walk to school, and parents spent more time at the neighborhood school. Now students were bused to a new school and those parents, grandparents, and caregivers did not have either cars to get to the new school or the money for bus or cab fare. Normally they would walk their children to and from the school each day. Since many of the students came from one-parent families, and with the adults working double shifts in order to make ends meet, there was little time left for caretakers to help the children with their homework, read to them, or teach them positive social skills and behaviors.

Mrs. T knew about a group of seniors who met at a family resource center in the neighborhood. Once a week, the seniors would have a potluck lunch, talk, laugh, and plan special informational programs. She knew they were aware of the problems in the neighborhood, but for some reason they had not taken any role in contributing to solutions to turn the neighborhood around. Mrs. T thought it might be worthwhile to explore ideas with this group to see if they would be interested in assisting the neighborhood children with the problems she saw in her class. The teacher decided, through her reading of the research, that an intergenerational project could be developed, based loosely on the ongoing program Across Ages, which had been proven successful in Philadelphia.

Mrs. T already had anecdotal records from school, standardized test scores, discipline referrals, and parent–teacher conference documentation. She decided to use this information for her baseline data.

Step 3: Design an Intervention

Mrs. T met with the seniors one day after school, and together they devised a plan to have the children work with the seniors on a number of issues: reading skills, life skills, and especially social skills. The teacher felt that if there was a concerted effort to target these three areas, the children would have a chance of improving all aspects of their educational progress. Once discussions got underway, Mrs. T learned that the seniors were not only willing but also excited about doing more for the neighborhood and its children. The children were already coming to the center after school, but there had not been any specific interventions for the children. While the after-school tutors had cited the lack of reading skills, and the necessity to build more positive life and social skills in the presence of adults, the help the children received was random and disconnected. One week the children would work with university students, the next a senior. No one was sharing information, nor was there a longitudinal look at each child.

Mrs. T decided to focus only on the eight students in her class who were from this targeted neighborhood and who needed these extra skills and interpersonal contacts, as identified from her records.

Step 4: Implement the Intervention

The seniors underwent a brief training period on how to provide positive tutoring to young people, and the children also had a brief training period to help them better understand older adults. Each child was paired with a senior.

The paired adults and children met two days a week for two hours after school. A variety of activities emerged from the interactions. Seniors read to the children, and children read to them. The seniors told stories of their childhoods or showed the children how to sew on buttons or braid hair. The seniors were especially skilled in tuning in to each child's needs. Sometimes the pair would take turns listening and telling about their lives. Mrs. T also asked that the families be scheduled to come in at the beginning so the seniors, children, and parents could meet. It became apparent after the first week that the seniors knew most of the families already.

Step 5: Collect Data from the Results of the Intervention

Mrs. T interviewed the seniors and the children at the middle and the end of the intervention. She asked the seniors the following questions:

- What kinds of activities are you doing with your child?
- How do you feel about working with this child?

- How do you feel about the opportunity to improve your child's academic performance, life skills, and social skills?
- What have been the rewards for you in taking on this activity?

The following questions were asked of the children:

- What kinds of activities are you doing with your special grandparent?
- How do you feel about working with this special grandparent?
- How well do you feel you read?
- How well do you feel you listen?
- What have you learned by working with your special grandparent?
- What is the best part of this program?

Step 6: Evaluate and Assess the Effectiveness of the Intervention

Mrs. T noted improvement in all three areas she had targeted. While not all eight children made significant gains in all three areas, all did improve. The most significant gains, though, were made in the life and social skills areas. Both seniors and children reported improved interactions with the children's peers. Mrs. T also noted a drop in the number of discipline referrals from this group and slight improvement in reading skills.

Step 7: Reflect on the Implications of the Intervention

Uprooting children who already have an unstable home life and busing them to a new school where they don't know many of their classmates only exacerbates the children's conditions of poverty. The supports, the familiarity of place, and the close connections between parents and school were severed when the children were bused to the new school. An already fragile community was made even more fragile.

The family resource center offered a place for children to go that provided an extended family atmosphere, where their special grandparents were always waiting to spend time with them—reading, talking, and showing them how to do new things.

Step 8: Reflect on the Overall Process

Mrs. T felt confident that with a new school to take pride in and enthusiastic teachers, the children would overcome any handicaps resulting from having attended their old neighborhood schools.

Mrs. T was pleased with the outcome of the intervention, even though it had a short life for the first research cycle. Based on the successes that came from this initial try at parent–child–community collaboration, the teacher decided to start up the program again next year with her new class. She felt that by starting earlier in the year, perhaps she would see even greater gains in children's academic achievement and social deportment.

Step 9: Begin the Cycle Again by Identifying a New or Continuing Area of Concern

Mrs. T, in reflecting on the whole process, realized that parents had played a minimal role. She began to think about ways to bring parents into the equation. Since the parents were working long hours, they usually did not have time to attend school functions or to become involved in the family resource center activities. Yet parental involvement would close the school–community–parent circle. Among her list of activities to include the following year were (1) finding opportunities for parents to participate without further stressing them and their workloads, (2) developing links to other community-based organizations (e.g., churches) to strengthen the work done by the seniors at the center, and (3) providing more opportunities for the children to better understand their special grandparents by visiting nursing homes and senior citizen centers.

Also, other questions emerged as she continued to reflect. What would happen if children were paired with adults in the neighborhood who needed and wanted literacy training? Would results be as good or better because of the interdependence of the pairs? Would more training for both child and senior further improve the outcomes, or was the initial training sufficient? How could she find ways to recognize the important work the seniors were doing and give them more support when they were feeling overwhelmed? Could Mrs. T begin to bridge the parent–child gap at school by having the seniors attend important events in the children's lives at school or even fill in at parent–teacher conferences?

REFERENCES

Freedman, M. (1988). *Partners in growth: Eldermentors and at-risk youth.* Philadelphia: Public/Private Ventures.

Taylor, A. S., & Dryfoos, J. G. (1998). Creating a safe passage: Elder mentors and vulnerable youth. *Generations, 22*(4), 43–49.

Townsel, K. T. (1997). Mentoring African American youth. *Preventing School Failure, 41*(3), 125–128.

Wolin, S., & Wolin, S. (1993). The challenge model: Discovering resiliency in children at risk. *Brown University Child and Adolescent Behavior Letter, 9*(3).

Conclusion

In the future, teachers will continue to face tremendous challenges to bring peace to the classroom. Cultural influences—including parenting styles, religious orientation, and the way social capital is built and utilized in various communities—will impact teachers and their ability to provide effective education for all students. It is therefore imperative that teachers become highly sophisticated in knowledge and understanding of these key cultural areas and how students' belief systems are molded by their ethnic, racial, linguistic, and religious backgrounds. Without sufficient knowledge of these cultural processes and how they influence child-rearing, teachers will struggle to provide effective programs for students.

We must be effective teachers with each and every child that comes into our classrooms. The ultimate goal of developing action research processes in pursuit of peaceful classrooms is to embed this pedagogical process into one's own teaching practice. This means that the cycle of plan-act-reflect should become as natural as the lesson-planning process, or any other type of pedagogical exercise that is repeated over time. In addition, peace-building processes should become a natural part of every lesson. Sustaining the action research process should not be any more difficult for teachers than sustaining any other classroom practice.

As can be seen from this book, reducing violence in classrooms is thoroughly influenced by the historical antecedents of our culture, its current manifestations, and the structural context within which these cultural processes are played out. For this reason, the book has explored the historical and cultural reasons behind violence in American society to give teachers a knowledge base and understanding about the foundations of our culture. By taking the legs of the stool—family, church, community—as originally conceived by the first Americans as the mode of cultural transmission, that is, education, the book has updated this concept to reflect the current cultural positioning of diverse families and how parenting styles produce social, life, and academic success. Community is looked at for how it can build social capital to support the success of its children, especially when poverty and violence have made fragile the cohesion of the community.

By studying the social context of the classroom first, teachers can determine if their practice attends to the needs of their diverse students. They can then accurately develop action research that will effectively manage problem behaviors in their classrooms. By situating their action research within the social context of the classroom, teachers can see what ideas are reasonable to pursue and those that are not addressed by current research. The realization that their problems are not represented in formal research should not discourage teachers but rather motivate them to move these agendas forward. Also, the idea of taking charge of one's own practice rather than using "canned" ideas should have a liberating effect. It is this practical knowledge that is at the heart and cutting edge of action research. Critical self-reflection and autonomy in designing teaching practices are key to the empowerment process.

I hope that this book has fostered additional awareness, examination, and consideration of the cultural contexts of violence prevention and the processes that can set effective classroom practice into motion. It is also hoped that the book will continue to invite discussions about these ideas and further development of the concepts herein. The book is meant to stimulate thinking about these issues and create a critical consciousness about the sources and resolutions of violence through active, effective processes.

Index

action research, 51–60; anecdotal records, 89; beginning cycle again, 59–60; checklists, 89–91, 93–94, 101; collecting information on problem, 52–54; data, collecting, 55–56; data, types of, 52, 53, 54–55; identifying concern, 52; observation, 79, 89; reflecting on effectiveness, 58–59; survey, 104

American values, 3–9; competitiveness, 5–6; family, church, community, 3–5; first generation, 3–5; formation of, 3–9; individualism, 6–7; materialism, 6–7; transmission of, 4–5, 7–8

art, 78, 79

classroom research. *See* action research

community, 39–47; building capacity of, 44; characteristics of, 39–41; collaboration and inclusion, 42–46; interaction, 42–46; levels of, 42–43; responsibility, 42–46; shared vision, 46; social capital, 41–42, 43, 44, 46; socially toxic, 46

conflict resolution, 62, 71–84

cooperative activities, 106–107, 109–110

cooperative groups, 99–114

discussion groups, 78, 79

families, 11–30, 32–34, 42–43, 44, 45

feedback, student, 79

force, use of to prevent violence, 61–62

games, 87

intervention: designing, 54–55; evaluating and assessing, 56–57; implementing, 55

literature, 77, 78, 79, 106

music, 78, 79

paired learning, 85–98

INDEX

parent–child–community collaboration, 115–122
parenting styles, 11–38; African, 17, 18; African American, 14, 17, 33; Asian Indians, 14, 18; authoritarian, 11–13, 32, 33; authoritative, 11–13, 21, 32–33; Chinese, 14–15; Hispanic, 13–14, 16, 19–20; intergenerational, 14, 15–19; Japanese, 17, 18; mainstream culture, 11–13, 21; Native American, 16–17, 18; permissive, 11–13; role of grandparents, 17, 18; Sudanese, 17; uninvolved, 12; variation among cultures, 14–15
peace: building, 61, 63–68; consciousness, 63; keeping, 61–62; making, 61, 62–63
peace processes, school-based, 61–69; administrative leadership, 64, 66; building content knowledge, 63, 65, 118–119; communication skills, 64, 71–84, 118–199; concept building, 64–65; creating conditions for sustained nonviolence, 63, 77–78, 80–81, 111, 118–119; curriculum, 63–68; Internet resources, 67–68; modeling responsible behavior, 64, 66, 118–199; motivating students, 64, 66, 71–84, 118–119; pedagogical techniques, 64, 66; proactive strategies, 62–63, 118–119; resources, 67–68; working with emotions, 63, 66, 71–84, 77, 78, 118–119
peer: learning, 85–98; mediation, 71–84
positive interdependence, 85–98
puzzles, 78, 79

reflective thinking activities, 71–84
religion and spirituality, 27–38; Buddhism, 28; Christianity, 28–29, 30–31, 31–32, 33–35; God images, 30–33; hard and soft, 27–28; Hindu, 27–28; Islam, 28; Judaism, 28; Occidental, 27–28, 30–32; Oriental, 27–28; related to parenting styles, 31–32; related to value orientations, 32–35; role of, 29–30
role-playing, 77, 78, 79

student behavior journals, 79

tolerance, promoting, 111

About the Author

Jean Benton is associate professor of social and cultural foundations of education at Southeast Missouri State University. Dr. Benton's scholarly work focuses on social and cultural forces in education, technology and cultural change, and education for social justice and self-determination. Among her publications are other books, such as *Creating Cultures of Peace: Pedagogical Thought and Practice,* book chapters, and articles published in Finnish and Russian journals. Dr. Benton works extensively with teachers and students in schools in the United States and abroad and has developed extensive study-abroad programs for all levels of undergraduate students in teacher education. She has been the recipient of EU-US FIPSE and Fulbright grants and has served on international boards and committees focusing on global and international teacher education policy issues. She received the Best Practice Award for Global and International Teacher Education from the American Association for Colleges of Teacher Education in 1999 and an Achievement Award from the World Council for Curriculum and Instruction in 2001.